BUILDING STRATEGIES

STRATEGIES 2

AN INTEGRATED LANGUAGE COURSE FOR LEARNERS OF ENGLISH

Brian Abbs
Ingrid Freebairn

Longman

TO THE STUDENT

Many of you have perhaps used our book 'Starting Strategies'. If so, you will already know how to introduce yourself, say where you are from, say what you do, talk about daily life and express other simple—but important—facts about yourself.

Now is the time to build up your language, to learn more words, more ways of saying things and more grammar so that you can say what you want to in many new situations.

In Building Strategies you will meet people who live in Bristol, a large city in the south west of England. As you read about them and as you study, you will learn how to narrate, report, describe, compare, instruct and exchange opinions. You will learn how to do these things in written as well as spoken English.

We hope you will enjoy this book; we hope that it will give you some strategies for successful communication; and we hope that it will give you a firm foundation on which to build your further study of English.

Brian Abbs,
Ingrid Freebairn,
London 1979

JACK COOPER is 53 years old. He is production manager at Weston Aeronautics. He is married to PEGGY and they have a daughter called BARBARA.

THE PEOPLE

ROD NELSON is a young electrical engineer from Ottawa in Canada.
He is in England working for a British company called Weston Aeronautics. He lives in a rented flat.

BARBARA COOPER is 24. She is the successful manageress of a shoe shop called 'Pretty Feet' in the centre of Bristol. She has a flat of her own in an old part of Bristol.

PAUL BLAKE is a student at Bristol Polytechnic. He studies maths and naval engineering. He shares a flat with ROD NELSON. His girlfriend, SUE, is also a student.

JOAN INGRAMS is a part-time secretary and housewife. She and her husband, NORMAN, live in a suburb of Bristol. They have two children, MARK and MANDY. They rent the upstairs part of their house to ROD NELS[...]

Bristol's waterfront: the cathedral on the left, and the commercial and business centre on the right.

Clifton: a beautiful eighteenth century terrace in the older part of Bristol.

A boat comes into Bristol on the River Avon under the Clifton Suspension Bridge.

THE PLACE

BRISTOL is a large city situated on the River Avon in the south west of England. It is an important commercial, tourist and shopping centre. Many visitors from all parts of the world come to Bristol to sight-see and to shop.

WESTON AERONAUTICS is a small company which makes electrical components for the British aircraft industry. It is situated on a new industrial estate in a suburb of Bristol.

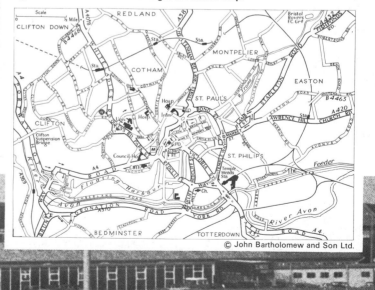

© John Bartholomew and Son Ltd.

Longman Group Limited
London

*Associated companies, branches and
representatives throughout the world*

© Longman Group Limited 1979

First published 1979
Second impression 1979
ISBN 0 582 51529 7

to those students and teachers
who have shared our enthusiasm
for and our belief in communicative
language teaching . . . .

*Printed in Great Britain by Spottiswoode Ballantyne Ltd.
Colchester and London*

CONTENTS

Gentlemen
Barbers
First Aid room
Police
Telephones

Tournament Buffe

A new start

1. Work in pairs. Ask your partner:

What's your name?
What nationality are you?
Where do you come from?
Where do you live?
What do you do?

Where do you $\begin{cases} \text{work?} \\ \text{study?} \end{cases}$

2. Work in groups. Talk about your partner.

His/Her name's.........
He's/She's.........
He/She comes from.........
He/She lives in.........
He's/She's a/an.........

He/She $\begin{cases} \text{works} \begin{cases} \text{in a......... in.......... } \\ \text{for......... } \end{cases} \\ \text{studies at......... } \end{cases}$

3. Fill in the dialogue.

Rod Nelson is in the buffet bar at Paddington Station in London. He is waiting for the train to Bristol. He looks for somewhere to sit down.

ROD: Excuse me, is this seat free?
ZLATKO: ....
ROD: You aren't English, are you?
ZLATKO: ....
ROD: Where do you come from in Yugoslavia?
ZLATKO: ....
ROD: Are you here on holiday?
ZLATKO: ....
ROD: My name's Rod, by the way. What's yours?
ZLATKO: ....
ROD: Would you like another coffee?
ZLATKO: ....
ROD: My train leaves in five minutes. I must go. Nice meeting you. Bye!
ZLATKO: ....

Use these responses to fill in the dialogue.

From Dubrovnik.
Goodbye.
Mine's Zlatko. Zlatko Tiric.
Yes, it is.
No, I'm not. I'm Yugoslavian.
No, thanks.
No, I'm not. I study in London.

Now listen to the dialogue and read it in pairs.

4. Roleplay

Imagine you are on holiday in Britain. This time _you_ are the person who meets Rod. In pairs, read the dialogue again.

PERSONAL INFORMATION RECORD	
NAME	My name is ....
NATIONALITY	I am ....
DOMICILE	I live in ....
	My address is ....
	....
	My telephone number is ....
OCCUPATION	I am a/an ....
STUDY DETAILS	I study English at ....
	I have studied English for .... months/terms/years.
	I want to learn English for:
	my job.
	my studies.
	travelling.
	pleasure and interest.
INTERESTS	I like .... in my spare time.

5. Fill in the personal information record.

6. Write 3 short paragraphs about yourself, your studies and your interests. Like this:

Name: Zlatko Tiric
Class: 2
Teacher: Mrs Williams

My name is Zlatko Tiric. I am Yugoslavian and I come from Dubrovnik. I live in a hostel in London. My address is: The International Hostel, 12 Bedford Square, London. My telephone number is 01-262-4136.

I am a student. I study English at the Regent School of English. I have studied English for a year. I want to learn English for my studies.

I like reading and going to discos in my spare time.

7. Listen to 3 people from different parts of Britain talking about where they live. The first speaker comes from London. Look at the notes about her.
Make similar notes about the other two people.
Write notes about yourself in the column marked YOU.

HOME	Jenny	David	Mary	YOU
a flat				
a house				
a hostel	student hostel			
a cottage				
LOCATION				
in a large town				
in a city	london- city			
in a suburb				
in a small town				
in a village				
in the country				
in the mountains				
near the sea				
GEOGRAPHICAL LOCATION				
in the / on the { N, NW, NE, W, E, SW, SE, S } of Britain / coast	south east of England			

8. Write a short paragraph about where you live. Read it to your partner.

Rod Nelson is a young electrical engineer from Ottawa in Canada. He is working in England for a company called Weston Aeronautics. The company makes electrical components. It is situated in Bristol, a large city in the south west of England.

Rod works with Jack Cooper, the production manager at Weston. Rod likes Jack and enjoys his job. He also likes England because it is so different from Canada. He lives in a hostel in Bristol but he wants to rent a flat of his own.

He started his job at Weston in September and a few weeks later he went to dinner at the Coopers' house. There he met Barbara. Barbara is Jack and Peggy Cooper's twenty-four year old daughter. She is the manageress of a shoe shop in the centre of Bristol. Rod doesn't know many people in Bristol so he enjoyed meeting her.

Who is Rod Nelson? *He's a young* ....

Where does he come from? *From* .... *in* ....

What does Weston Aeronautics make? *It makes* ....

Where is it situated? *In* ...., *a large* .... *in the* .... *of England.*

What does Jack Cooper do? *He's the* .... *at Weston.*

Does Rod like his job at Weston? ...., *he* ....

Why does he like England? *Because it's so* .... *from* ....

Where does he live? *In a* ....

Where does he want to live? *In a* .... *of his* ....

When did he start his job at Weston? *In* ....

When did he meet Barbara? *A few* ....

Who is Barbara? *She's* .... *and* .... *'s* ....

Where did he meet Barbara? *He met her at dinner at the* ....

How old is she? *She's* ....

What does she do? *She's the* .... *of a* ....

Why did Rod enjoy meeting her? *Because he* .... *many people* ...... *Bristol.*

* * *

What do you know about:
Rod Nelson?
Jack Cooper?
Weston Aeronautics?
Barbara?
Where and when did Rod meet Barbara?

Link your sentences using *and, but, so* **and** *because.*

Oral Exercises

1. Ask where people come from

I'm Canadian.
Oh, yes. Where in Canada do you come from?
She's English.
Oh, yes. Where in England does she come from?

I'm Canadian.
She's English.
He's Yugoslavian.
They're Italian.
I'm French.
She's Australian.

2. Ask where people live

Rod works in Bristol.
Oh, does he live there too?

I study in Bristol.
Oh, do you live there too?

Rod works in Bristol.
I study in Bristol.
Barbara has a shop in Bristol.
Paul studies in Bristol.
My parents both work in Bristol.

3. Say where places and things are

It is Rod's first day at Weston Aeronautics.
Jack Cooper is showing him around.

ROD: Where's *your* office, by the way?
JACK: *That's mine, over there.*
ROD: Oh, yes. And where's *my* room?
JACK: *That's yours over there.*

ROD: Where's *your* office, by the way?
Oh, yes. And where's *my* room?
And what about Mike's office?
And the secretary? Where's hers?
Oh, yes. Oh—where's my desk, by the way?
And what about yours?

4. Give correct information

Rod cannot find where places and things are.

ROD: Is that Jack's office?
GIRL: *No, Jack's office is here.*
ROD: I see. And this is the secretary's room, isn't it?
GIRL: *No, the secretary's room is here.*

Is that Jack's office?
I see. And this is the secretary's room, isn't it?
Oh, yes. And is that Mike's office?

Ah! Now, I'd like to make a phone call.
Is this the secretary's telephone?
But this is John's office?

5. Give reasons

Why do you live in Bristol?
Because I like living in Bristol.
Why do you always get up early?
Because I like getting up early.

Why do you live in Bristol?
Why do you always get up early?
Why do you always cycle to work?
Why do you always go to bed early?
Why do you always study at night?
Why do you write letters every day?

6.*Answer these questions about yourself

What's your name?
What nationality are you?
Where do you come from?
Where do you live?
What do you do?
Where do you work or study?

Open Dialogue

Talk to Rod. You meet in the canteen at Weston Aeronautics.

ROD: Hi! My name's Rod. What's yours?
YOU: ....
ROD: You aren't English, are you?
YOU: ....
ROD: Where exactly do you come from?
YOU: ....
ROD: What part of the country is that in?
YOU: ....
ROD: Oh, yes. I live in a hostel at the moment. What about you?
YOU: ....
ROD: Anyway, what do you like doing in your spare time?
YOU: ....
ROD: I see. And why do you want to learn English?
YOU: ....
ROD: Well, that's a good reason. Where do you study, by the way?
YOU: ....
ROD: Oh, there's a friend of mine over there. I'd like to talk to her. It was nice meeting you. Bye!
YOU: ....

CHECK

Now you can:

1. Give personal information about yourself and others

My name's Zlatko.
I'm Yugoslavian.
I come from Dubrovnik.
I'm a student.
I live in a hostel in London.
My address/telephone number is …

2. Describe where places are

It is situated in Bristol, a large city in the south west of England.

3. Link sentences with *and*, *but*, *so* and *because*

He likes Jack *and* enjoys his job.
He lives in a hostel, *but* he wants to find a flat.
He likes England *because* it's different from Canada.
He doesn't know many people, *so* he enjoyed meeting Barbara.

Grammar

This is	my your his her	house.

It's	mine. yours. his. hers.

This is	Jack's room. Rod's flat. the Coopers' house.

I'm a student *so* I haven't got a lot of money.
I haven't got a lot of money *because* I'm a student.
I live in a hostel *so* I haven't got a telephone number.
I haven't got a telephone number *because* I live in a hostel.

Words and phrases

seat	production	come from	different	That's very kind of you!
cottage	manager	enjoy	situated	
city	manageress	meet/met	electrical	
village	shoe shop	know	another	
mountain	daughter	rent		
coast	interest		so	
spare time	pleasure	mine	because	
component		of mine		
		yours		
		his		
		hers		

At the Coopers' house before dinner.

BARBARA: Do you like working at Weston, Rod?

ROD: Yes, very much. The job's interesting and the people there are very friendly.

BARBARA: And do you mind living in a hostel?

ROD: It's all right, but I want to find a flat of my own soon. Where do you live, by the way?

BARBARA: In a flat on the other side of the city, in an old part of Bristol. What do you think of Bristol?

ROD: I like it. It's a beautiful city and the countryside around here is lovely. How do *you* like Bristol?

BARBARA: Well, it's my home town, of course. I think it's a bit depressing in winter, but it's nice in spring and autumn. Do you know many people yet?

ROD: No, not many. Unfortunately.

BARBARA: Well, would you like to come and have a look round the shoe shop one day? In fact, what about coming next Saturday at lunch time? We close at one o'clock.

ROD: Thanks. That's a great idea. Why don't we have lunch together?

BARBARA: Fine. I'm not so keen on big lunches, but we could have something light.

ROD: Good. That's fixed, then.

PEGGY: Come on, you two. Dinner's ready.

Making

Does Rod like his job at Weston? ......, he ....

Where does he live? *In a* ....

Where does Barbara live? *In a* ...., *on* .... side of the city, in an ....

Does Rod know many people in Bristol? ......, he ....

What does Barbara invite Rod to do? *To* .... and have a .... the ....

When does she suggest? *Next* .... at .... o'clock.

What does Rod suggest they do? *Have* .... together.

SET 1   **Express likes and dislikes**

Do you like cooking?	Yes, very much.
	It's all right.
	Sometimes. It depends.
	No, not much.
	No, I hate it.
Do you mind doing housework?	
	No, I like it.
	It's all right.
	Sometimes. It depends.
	Yes, I hate it.

1. Work in pairs. Ask your partner about his/ her likes and dislikes. Write down his/her answers.

Your partner's answers

Do you like...?
  cooking
  going for long walks
  sightseeing
  swimming
  dancing
  reading

Do you mind...?
  writing letters
  washing up
  doing housework
  ironing
  going to work
  getting up early
  staying at home on
    Saturday night
  being on your own

friends

What sort of lunch does Barbara suggest? *A .... lunch.*

* * *

What does Rod think of his job at Weston? *He thinks it's ....*

What does he think of the people there? *He thinks they're ....*

What does he think of living in a hostel? *He thinks it's .... but ....*

What does he think of Bristol?

What does he think of the countryside?

What does Barbara think of Bristol?

2. Write a few lines about your partner's likes and dislikes. Like this:

Maria likes reading and sightseeing very much, but she doesn't like cooking or doing housework. On the other hand, she doesn't mind getting up early or being on her own.

3. Now write a few lines about yourself. Like this:

I like .... and ...., but ....

SET 2 Express personal opinions

Do you like working at Weston, Rod?
Yes, very much. The job's interesting and the people there are very friendly.

What do you think of the new theatre?

I think it's awful.

Do you? I think it's quite attractive. What do you think Ann?

I don't like it. I think it's ugly.

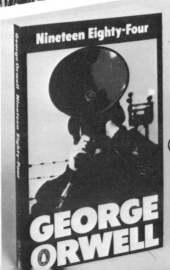

How do you like the people here?

They're all right. They're very friendly, but they're a bit old fashioned.

Do you like this book?

I don't know. It's fascinating, but it's also a bit depressing.

Nineteen Eighty-Four

GEORGE ORWELL

Ask for an opinion

What do you think of ...?

How do you like ...?

Do you like ...?

Express an opinion

I think it's ...
 they're ...
 he's ...
 etc.
I think he/she/it looks ...
I like it. It's ...
It's all right but ...
I don't like it. I think it's ...
Yes/No/I don't know. It's ...

Words to use

lovely awful
marvellous boring
interesting dull
fascinating depressing
attractive ugly
friendly unfriendly
beautiful old-fashioned
modern (over)crowded

1. **Work in pairs. Ask and answer about the
 places, people and things you can see in the
 pictures above, like this:**

 What do you think of that man?
 I think he looks interesting.

🔾🔾

2. **Listen to 4 people saying what they think of
Britain. Make notes about what they say.**

	THE WEATHER	THE FOOD	THE PEOPLE AND THE WAY OF LIFE
 Paul comes from Jamaica	*miserable, cold, damp, changeable depressing*	*rather boring, no flavour, no taste*	*old people-snobbish young people-alive on fire, free*
 Cindy comes from Los Angeles, U.S.A.			
 Usha comes from Madras, India.			
 Spiro comes from Salonika, Greece.			

🔾🔾

3. **Roleplay**

Work in pairs. Imagine that your partner is a visitor *either* to your country *or* to Britain. Ask his/her opinions about some of these things:

the weather   the food   the people
the way of life   the countryside   the houses
some famous buildings

Make notes of your partner's answers.

4. **Write a few sentences about your partner's opinions. Like this:**

Maria thinks the weather is nice in summer, <u>but</u> awful in winter, <u>and</u> she doesn't like the food very much. <u>On the other hand</u>, she thinks the people here are very friendly and she likes the way of life. She thinks that the houses are dull, <u>but</u> some of the famous buildings, like Westminster Abbey, are very beautiful.

SET 3 **Make suggestions and plans**
Agree and disagree with suggestions

What about coming next Sunday?	That's a good idea!
How about meeting for lunch?	That's a great idea!
Why don't we have lunch together?	Well, I'm not so keen on lunch. How about supper instead?

1. Make a list of things to do and places to go to in your area. Make 2 suggestions for:

Places to have a meal	Films or plays to go to see	Places of interest to go to	Sports or activities to watch or play

2. Work in pairs. Ask and answer like this:

What about having a meal at ...?
or How about going to see ...?
      going to ...?
      watching/playing some ...?
Yes, that's a good/great idea!

3. Work in pairs. Ask and answer like this:

Why don't we have a meal at ...?
      go to see ...?
      go to ...?
      watch/play some ...?
Well, I'm not so keen on .... Why don't we ...... instead?

4. Work in groups. Make suggestions and plans for:

   1) a day trip to somewhere interesting.
   2) an evening out in your nearest town.

Plan where to go/what to do/when to meet/ what food to take/how to get there.

Oral Exercises

1.* Say what *you* like doing

What sort of things do you like doing in summer?
I like (walking and playing tennis).

What do you like doing at home when it's raining?
I like (reading).

What sort of things do you like doing in summer?
What do you like doing at home when it's raining?
What sort of things do you like reading?
What do you like doing when you go out at the weekends?
What things do you like doing when you go out in the evening?
What sort of jobs do you like doing in your home?

2.* Express likes and dislikes

Do you mind getting up early?
(Yes, I do, I hate it.)

What about in the summer? Do you mind getting up early then?
(Sometimes. It depends.)

Do you mind doing housework?
(No, I don't, I like it.)

Do you mind getting up early?
What about the summer? Do you mind getting up early then?
Do you mind doing housework?
Do you mind people smoking when you are eating?
Do you mind people talking when you are watching TV?
Do you mind travelling in the rush hour?
Do you mind doing homework?
Do you mind waiting for other people?

3. Ask if people mind doing things
A friend is thinking of becoming a policeman.

The police have to work long hours.
Well, yes. Do you mind working long hours?

They have to do shift work as well.
Well, yes. Do you mind doing shift work?

The police have to work long hours.
They have to do shift work as well.
They have to wear a uniform too.
And they have to work at night.
The police tell people what to do.

4.* Ask for and give opinions

Ask Rod what he thinks of the weather.
YOU: *What do you think of the weather?*
ROD: It's all right, but it rains a lot. How do you like the weather in your country?
YOU: *(I like it. It's very hot in summer.)*

Ask Rod what he thinks of English food.
YOU: *What do you think of English food?*
ROD: I think it's fantastic. What do you think of the food in your country?
YOU: *(It's all right, but it's a bit dull.)*

Ask Rod what he thinks of the weather.
Ask Rod what he thinks of English food.
Ask him what he thinks of the way of life in England.
Ask him what he thinks of the people.
Ask him what he thinks of the modern buildings.

5. Make suggestions

I'd like to go to the cinema this week.
Well, how about going on Monday?

And I'd like to eat out some time too.
Well, how about eating out on Tuesday?

I'd like to go to the cinema this week.
And I'd like to eat out some time too.
Can't we go to the theatre one evening?
Why don't we ever drive into the country?
I'd like to visit my parents one day.
And we never play tennis together now.

6.* Disagree with a suggestion and make your own suggestion
Look at page 12 to help you with your own suggestions.

What about going to see a horror film this evening?
I'm not so keen on horror films. Why don't we see (Love Story) instead?

Let's have some Chinese food first.
I'm not so keen on Chinese food. Why don't we have some (Italian) food instead?

What about going to see a horror film this evening?
Let's have some Chinese food first.
What about going swimming tomorrow?
Or shall we watch TV?
And then let's have fish for supper.
How about going to the country for the weekend?

EXTENSION

Are you the right person for the job?

So you want to be:

a nurse?
an architect?
a computer operator?
a hairdresser?
a travelling
representative?
an air steward or
stewardess?
a travel guide?
a policeman or
policewoman?
a technician?

Features of the job

Do you like …?	Do you mind …?
meeting people	working at night
driving	doing shift work
working with children	working outside
telling people what to do	wearing a uniform
talking	working long hours
travelling	working on your own
looking after people	working in an office

1. Write down the title of each job. Write 3 questions for each job. Work in pairs. Interview your partner and find out which job would suit him/her best. Like this:

   (A nurse)
   Do you mind working at night?
   Do you like looking after people?
   Do you mind wearing a uniform?

Making a New Start

by Mike Sanders

EVERY week Mike Sanders meets people who are making a new start in life. This week Mike meets Rod Nelson, a young Canadian . . .

Rod comes from Ottawa and is an electrical engineer. He first trained at a college of engineering and then worked for the Canadian government. Last month he arrived in Britain to start a new job with Weston Aeronautics, a small company here in Bristol, which makes electrical components for the British aircraft industry.

Why did you leave Canada?
I was bored. I worked in the same office and saw the same people and did the same thing every day. I needed a change.

Why did you choose Bristol?
I saw some photographs of Bristol. It looked attractive. I like old cities and I like being near the sea.

What do you think of Bristol?
I like the people very much. They're very friendly. The way of life is different from Canada. It's a bit slow, perhaps, but I like it. And I love the food here, the fresh cream and the marvellous cheeses.

Have you any plans for the future?
No, not yet. I enjoy working at Weston and—well, I'm not so keen on making plans.

2.
Where did Rod first train as an engineer? *At a* .... *of* ....
Who did he work for in Canada? *For the* ....
When did he arrive in Britain? .... *month.*
Does he have any plans for the future? ......, *he* .... *Not* ....
Why not? *Because he's not keen* .... *plans.*

Why did Rod leave Canada? *He left because* ....
Why did he choose Bristol? *He chose Bristol because* .... *and it* ....
What does he think of Bristol? *He* .... *the people and thinks they* ....

3. **Write a short composition about Rod Nelson. Write 4 paragraphs using the facts from the newspaper article.**
    Paragraph 1 Say who Rod Nelson is and why he is in England.
    Paragraph 2 Say why he left Canada.
    Paragraph 3 Say why he chose to come to Bristol.
    Paragraph 4 Say what he thinks of Bristol.

4. **Roleplay**
    It is a hot Saturday in summer. Telephone a friend and plan the day.

YOU	YOUR FRIEND
	Answer the phone. Say your name.
Greet your friend and say your name.	
	Return greeting.
Suggest something to do in the afternoon.	
	Disagree. Make another suggestion.
Agree. Suggest a time and place to meet.	
	Agree. Say goodbye.
Say goodbye.	

CHECK

Now you can:

1. Ask about people's likes and dislikes

Do you like swimming?
Do you mind cooking?

2. Say how much you like or dislike things

Yes, very much.
No, not much.
It's all right.
Sometimes, it depends.
I like/hate it.

3. Ask for opinions

What do you think of …?
How do you like …?
Do you like …?

4. Express opinions

I think it's …
I think he looks …
I like it. It's …

5. Make suggestions and plans

What about going to …?
How about going to …?
Why don't we go to …?

6. Agree and disagree

That's a good idea.
Fine!
That's a great idea!
I'm not so keen on swimming.

Grammar

Do you	like mind	cooking? doing housework?

I don't	like mind	sightseeing.
I'm not so keen on		writing letters.

What How	about	having a meal at Franco's? going to see Star Wars? watching some football?

Why don't we	have a meal at Franco's? go to see Star Wars? watch some football?

I think	it's he's she's they're	interesting. lovely. attractive.

I think	it he she	looks	friendly.
	they	look	unfriendly.

Words and phrases

countryside	airsteward(ess)	great	depressing	very	train
winter	travel guide	alone	marvellous	not much	wash up
spring	shift work	long	slow	or	think of
summer	uniform	dull	same	the other side of	hate
autumn	way of life	unfriendly	other	on the other hand	have a look round
computer operator	change	ugly			need
nurse	trip	attractive	unfortunately	fish	it depends
architect		old-fashioned	a bit	organise	choose
policeman (woman)		overcrowded	perhaps	look after	

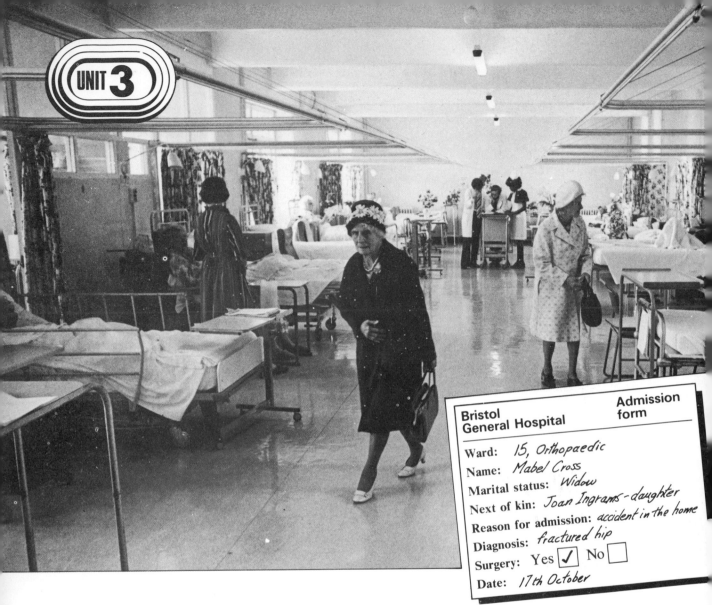

Bristol General Hospital — Admission form

Ward: 15, Orthopaedic
Name: Mabel Cross
Marital status: Widow
Next of kin: Joan Ingrams - daughter
Reason for admission: accident in the home
Diagnosis: fractured hip
Surgery: Yes ✓ No ☐
Date: 17th October

Ward Fifteen

Joan Ingrams is a part-time secretary and housewife. She and her family live in a house outside Bristol. Their house is quite large, so last week they found someone to rent the upstairs part of it—Rod Nelson, in fact.

Joan's mother, Mrs Cross, is a widow. She lives in a small cottage in a village in the country outside Bristol. Last week she had an accident. She fell down the stairs and broke her hip. She is now in hospital. Joan went to see her after the operation.

In Ward 15

JOAN: Hello, mum. How do you feel today?
MRS CROSS: Not too good, I'm afraid.
JOAN: Oh dear, I *am* sorry. What's the matter?
MRS CROSS: I don't know, but I've got a pain in my back now.
JOAN: Well, why don't you tell the nurse?
MRS CROSS: Yes, I will. Now how are the children?
JOAN: Oh, Mark has got a cold and a slight temperature. But he's a little better today. And Mandy's very well.
MRS CROSS: Oh, I am glad.
JOAN: Did you sleep well last night?

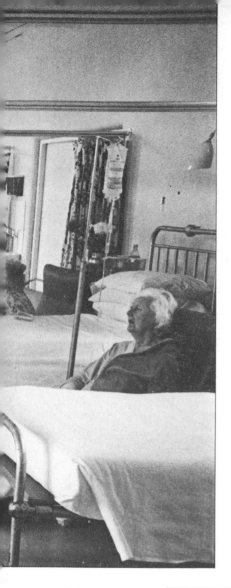

MRS CROSS : No, I didn't, I'm afraid. Old Mrs Grey in the next bed snored all night.
JOAN : Ssh! Mum!
MRS CROSS : Did you have a nice weekend? The weather was lovely.
JOAN : Yes, we did. We went for a walk in the country and Mandy went swimming. Oh, and we found someone for the upstairs flat. A young Canadian. He's very nice.
MRS CROSS : Oh, that's good.
JOAN : I must go back now and look after Mark. He's still got a temperature. Norman's at work, of course.
MRS CROSS : All right, dear. Give them all my love.
JOAN : I will. See you tomorrow.

Who is Joan Ingrams? *She's a .... and ....*

Where do the Ingrams live? *In a ....*

Why did they want to rent the upstairs part of their house? *Because .... quite ....*

Who did they find?

Who is Mrs Cross? *She's ....'s ....*

Does Mrs Cross live alone? *......, because she's a ....*

How old is she?

Where does she live? *In a .... in a .... in the .... outside Bristol.*

Why is Mrs Cross in hospital? *Because she .... the stairs and .... her hip.*

What are the names of Joan's husband and children?

Why must Joan go back home? *Because Mark has .... and she must .... him.*

* * *

How does Mrs Cross feel? *Not ....*

What's the matter with her now? *She's got ....*

What's the matter with Mark? *He's got ....*

How is Mandy? *She's ....*

Did Mrs Cross sleep well last night? *......, she ....*

What was the weather like last weekend? *It ....*

What did the Ingrams do at the weekend? *They went .... and Mandy ....*

SET 1 Discuss personal comfort and health
Sympathise and make suggestions

How do you feel today?	Much better, thanks.	Oh, good!
How's your headache?	A little better, thanks.	Oh, I *am* glad.
How's your back?	Not too bad, thanks.	
	Not too good, I'm afraid.	Oh dear, I *am* sorry.

1. Work in pairs. Ask, answer and respond like this:

   How do you feel today?
   Much better, thanks.
   Oh, good!
   or
   How's your back?
   Not too good, I'm afraid.
   Oh, dear, I *am* sorry.

What's the matter?   I've got a headache.   I feel sick.
                     a stomachache.   ill.
                     a bad cold.   awful.
                     a temperature.
                     a pain in my back.
                              shoulder.
                              leg.

Oh, dear. I *am* sorry. Why don't you lie down?
                              take an aspirin?
                              go home?
                              see a doctor?

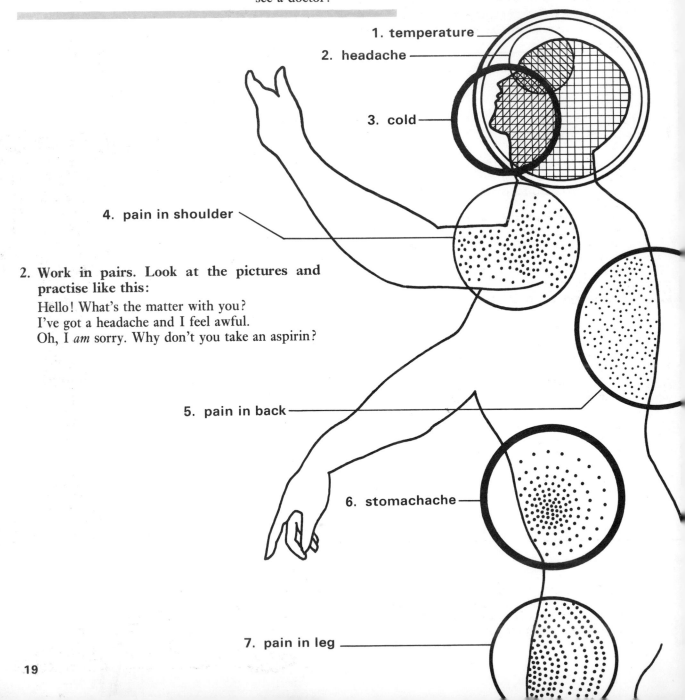

1. temperature

2. headache

3. cold

4. pain in shoulder

2. **Work in pairs. Look at the pictures and practise like this:**

Hello! What's the matter with you?
I've got a headache and I feel awful.
Oh, I *am* sorry. Why don't you take an aspirin?

5. pain in back

6. stomachache

7. pain in leg

SET 2   Ask and talk about the recent past

Did you have more than two pieces of bread for breakfast?

Yes, I did. I had three.   No, I didn't. I only had one.

1. Think about yesterday...
Work in pairs. Do the questionnaire. Fill in *your own* and *your* partner's answers. Then check your scores.

How healthy are you?

	YOU	YOUR PARTNER	SCORE	
			YES	NO
CHECK YOUR DIET				
Yesterday . . .				
1. Did you have more than two pieces of toast for breakfast?			0	1
2. Did you have sugar in your tea or coffee?			0	1
3. Did you drink half a litre of milk?			1	0
4. Did you eat any fruit?			1	0
5. Did you eat any sweets or chocolates?			0	1
6. Did you eat any biscuits or cake?			0	1
7. Did you drink any alcohol?			0	1
CHECK YOUR CONDITION				
Yesterday . . .				
8. Did you go for a run?			1	0
9. Did you do any exercises?			1	0
10. Did you walk or cycle to work/school?			1	0
11. Did you smoke at all?			0	1
CHECK YOUR DAILY ROUTINE				
Yesterday . . .				
12. Did you get up before 8 o'clock?			1	0
13. Did you go to bed before 11 o'clock?			1	0
14. Did you watch TV for more than 2 hours?			0	1
15. Did you sleep with your windows open?			1	0
TOTAL				

How did you score?
***15–12 Congratulations! You are very healthy—but don't forget to relax!
*12–8 Not too bad! Keep trying!
8–0 Oh dear! Oh dear!

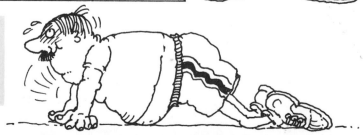

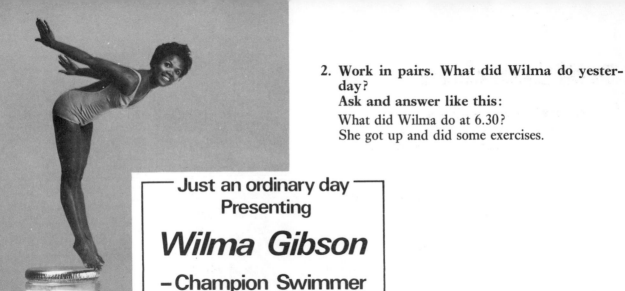

2. Work in pairs. What did Wilma do yesterday?
Ask and answer like this:
What did Wilma do at 6.30?
She got up and did some exercises.

Just an ordinary day
Presenting

Wilma Gibson

– Champion Swimmer

Morning
6.30 I get up and do some exercises.
7.00 I have a glass of milk and then I
        go for a run in the park.
8.00 I have breakfast with my husband.
        I have orange juice, an egg, bread
        and butter and a cup of tea with
        lemon.
9.15 I go to the pool and swim until
        lunchtime.

Afternoon
14.30 I teach swimming at the local school.
16.00 I have a glass of milk and some fruit.
        Then I go home, do some housework
        and relax.

Evening
19.00 We have a light supper.
        Then we watch television. I go to bed
        about ten o'clock. But I always have
        a glass of milk first!

3. Write a composition about Wilma's day. Start like this:
Yesterday Wilma Gibson, the swimming champion, got up at half past six and did some exercises. Then she …

Link your sentences with '*and*' or '*and then*'.
Start new sentences with '*Then she*' or '*After breakfast/lunch/school/supper she …*'

4. Write a composition about your day yesterday.

5. Work in pairs. Talk to your partner about recent past events. Use the table.

Did you have	a good time an interesting holiday an enjoyable party a good day out	last night? last weekend? last week? last month?

Yes,		did.		marvellous great lovely	time. holiday. party. day out.
No,	I/We	didn't.	I/We had a/an	boring miserable awful	

Oh, really?	What did you do? Where did you go? What happened?

Oral Exercises

1. **Say what's wrong with you**
Look at the picture on page 19.

1 What's the matter with you? You don't look very well.
I've got a temperature.
Oh, dear. Why don't you take an aspirin?

2 What's the matter?
I've got a headache.
Well, why don't you go to bed?

1 What's the matter with you? You don't look very well.
2 What's the matter?
3 You don't look too good. What's the matter?
4 You look awful. What's the matter?
5 What's the matter?
6 What's the matter with you? Are you all right?
7 What's the matter with you? Can't you walk?

2.* **Sympathise and make suggestions**
Sympathise in any way you wish and make a suitable suggestion.

I've got a headache.
(Oh, I am sorry. Why don't you take an aspirin and lie down?)

Barbara's got an awful cold.
(Oh, dear! Why doesn't she stay in bed today?)

I've got a headache.
Barbara's got an awful cold.
I feel awful. My head aches. I think I've got a temperature.
Rod says that he can't sleep at night.
Jack's got an awful pain in his back.
I don't know what's the matter with me. I've got an awful stomachache.

3.* **Answer questions about the recent past**
Answer the questions in any way you wish.

Did you go to bed early last night?
(Yes, I did. I went to bed at ten o'clock.)

Did you have a good breakfast this morning?
(No, I didn't. I only had a cup of tea.)

Did you go to bed early last night?
Did you have a good breakfast this morning?
Did you have an English lesson yesterday?
Did you do any shopping yesterday?
Did you watch television yesterday?
Did you do anything interesting last weekend?

4. **Answer questions about Wilma Gibson's day**
Look at page 21.

Did Wilma stay in bed until seven o'clock?
No, she got up and did some exercises at half past six.

What did she do after that?
She had a glass of milk and then went for a run in the park.

Did Wilma stay in bed until seven o'clock?
What did she do after that?
Did she have breakfast alone?
What did she do after breakfast?
What did she do after lunch?
What did she have to eat and drink at four o'clock?
What did she do at home between four o'clock and supper time?
What did she and her husband do after supper?

5.* **Answer questions about your daily activities**

What time did you get up this morning?
I got up at (6.30).

What time did you go to bed last night?
I went to bed at (11 o'clock).

What time did you get up this morning?
What time did you go to bed last night?
What time did you leave home this morning?
What time did you get home yesterday?
What time did you finish work yesterday?
What time did you arrive here today?
What time did you have supper yesterday?

6. **Ask for details about the recent past**

I watched TV last night.
Really? What did you watch?

I went to the theatre last week.
Really? What did you see?

I watched TV last night.
I went to the theatre last week.
I went to the cinema yesterday.
I bought a beautiful present for my mother yesterday.
I saw a friend of yours in town yesterday.
I had a marvellous meal last night.
We went to a marvellous place for our holidays.

EXTENSION

1. Roleplay

A friend comes to see you on Saturday morning. You feel awful—you have got a bad cold and a temperature.

2. Work in pairs. Imagine your partner is in hospital. You decide to visit him/her. Think of:

3 questions to ask your partner
3 interesting things to tell your partner (about yourself, what you did at the weekend, local events etc.)

Now act out a conversation with your partner.

Use phrases like:

By the way,
   I.........   Oh, did you?
   we.........   Oh, yes?
   did you know, I.........?   That's interesting.
                         Really?

YOUR FRIEND	YOU
	Open door and greet friend.
Greet and ask what's the matter.	
	Say what's the matter.
Say you are sorry and suggest something.	
	Agree to do this. Ask friend to post a letter.
Agree. Say you will come again tomorrow.	
	Thank friend and say goodbye.

3. Listening

A reporter is talking to some athletes about their training programmes. Listen and complete the chart.

	Bo Lundquist Swedish cyclist	Anne Cole British swimmer	Bob Maley American long-distance runner
Gets up at			
Starts training at			
Finishes training at			
Spare time activities			

Now write Anne and Bob's diary for yesterday.
Start like this:

Diary   Saturday 9th August

Yesterday I got up at

CHECK

Now you can:

1. Ask about personal comfort and health

How do you feel today?
How's your headache?
What's the matter?

2. Talk about personal comfort and health

I've got a cold.
I feel sick.
(I'm) much better, thanks.
(I'm) not too well, I'm afraid.

3. Express pleasure or sympathy

Oh, good!
Oh, I *am* glad.
Oh, dear. I *am* sorry.

4. Make suitable suggestions

Why don't you see a doctor?

5. Ask about the recent past

Did you have a nice weekend?
What did you do?

6. Talk about the recent past

I went for a walk.
I stayed at home.

7. Link past events

I got up at six. Then I did some exercises.
After breakfast I went …

Grammar

How	do / does	you / he / she	feel today?

I've / He's / She's	got	a bad cold. / a temperature. / a pain in my/his/her back.

What's the matter with	you? / him? / her?

I / He / She	feel / feels	sick. / awful. / ill.

What did	you / he / she / they	do? / see? / have?

I / He / She / They	went for a walk. / saw an old film on television. / had a glass of milk.

Words and phrases

widow
accident
stairs
hip
operation
pain
back
cold
headache
stomachache

temperature
leg
shoulder
aspirin
piece
sweet
alcohol
swimming pool

glad
sick
healthy
miserable
better

until
first
then
after

feel
look
break
relax
snore

TWO SUBURBS

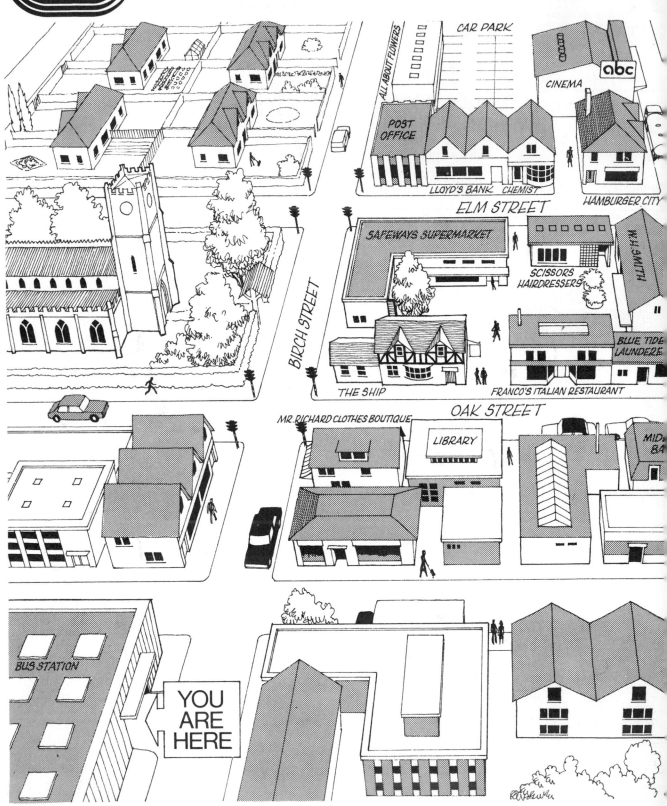

 SET 1 Ask and talk about facilities

Is there a swimming pool in Portland?	Yes, there is.
Is there a railway station?	No, there isn't.
Are there any restaurants?	Yes, there are. There are three altogether.
Are there any tennis courts?	No, there aren't.

1. **Work in pairs. Look at the map of Portland. Ask and answer about these facilities:**

a chemist	pubs
a disco	nightclubs
a supermarket	restaurants
a travel agency	banks
a theatre	a hairdresser
a park	a post office
a museum	a football ground
a swimming pool	a railway station
a church	a library

Is there a post office near here?	Yes, there's one on the corner of Elm Street and Birch Street.
Is there a bank near here?	Yes, there are two. There's one in Elm Street next to the post office. And one on the corner of Oak Street and Poplar Street.

2. **Work in pairs. Look at the map. Ask and say where places are in Portland.**

TWO SUBURBS: PORTLAND THE NEW SUTTON THE OLD

PORTLAND is a new suburb three miles east of Bristol with a population of about 25,000. It is a well-planned, modern suburb of the eighties. As well as the essential services, such as a shopping centre, a post office, banks, schools and a good bus service, there is also a library, a swimming pool and a cinema. There are also some good pubs and restaurants.

There is something for everybody in Portland.

SUTTON—A SUBURB OF THE PAST

Sutton, a suburb north of Bristol, with a population of about 19,000, is a typical example of a post-war, badly planned suburb. The population is large, but the essential services and the cultural, entertainments and sports facilities are poor.

Except for a few shops, a bank, a post office and a school, there are not many facilities in Sutton. There is nothing for people to do in their spare time. For example, there is no library, no cinema, no swimming pool. There are no parks or playground; there isn't even a good restaurant.

What do people do in their spare time in Sutton? Joan Little, a 22-year-old secretary, says: 'Nothing! There's nothing to do in Sutton. People stay at home and watch TV.'

Yes, Sutton IS a badly-planned suburb. And there are many suburbs like this near Bristol. So take note, Bristol Council. We need more suburbs like Portland, more well-planned places to live in, places which satisfy the needs of a living community.

Where is Portland situated? .... of Bristol.
What is the population? *About* .... *thousand.*
Is it a well-planned suburb?
Where is Sutton situated? .... of Bristol.
How many people live there? *About* ....
What do people do in their spare time in Sutton? .... *They* .... *at home and* ....
Is Sutton well-planned? ......, *it's* .... *planned.*
Are there any other suburbs like this?

* * *

What essential services are there in Portland? *There's a* .... *and a* .... *and there are* .... *and* ....
What facilities are there for spare time activities? *There's a* .... *and there are* ....
What essential services are there in Sutton? *There's only a* ....
Why do people in Sutton have nothing to do in their spare time? *Because there's no* ....

---

3. Mike Sander, the journalist who interviewed Rod, writes about two suburbs of Bristol.

As well as the essential services, there is also a library.

4. Link these sentences together with *as well as.*

There is a swimming pool. There is also a theatre.
There is a good shopping centre. There are also some small shops.
There are good entertainment facilities. There is also a library.

Except for a few shops, a bank, a post office and a school, there are not many facilities in Sutton.

5. Link these sentences with *except for.*

There is a swimming pool. There are no other sports facilities.
There is a cinema. There is no other form of entertainment.
There is a bus service. There is no other form of transport.

6. Work in groups. Discuss the facilities and services in your areas.
Like this:

Is there a good bus/train/underground service?
What sports facilities are there?
What cultural and entertainment facilities are there?
There's ....   There's no ....
There are ....   There are no ....
As well as ...., there's/there are ....
Except for ...., there's no/there are no ....

One Friday, Rod drove out to Portland on business. Then he realised that he needed some money for the weekend. So he parked his car near the bus station.

ROD: Excuse me. Is there a bank near here?

MAN: Yes, the nearest one is in Oak Street.

ROD: I'm afraid I'm a stranger here. How do I get to Oak Street?

MAN: You walk down Birch Street as far as the first traffic lights. Then you turn right and the bank is at the end of the street on the right. In fact it's on the corner of Oak Street and Poplar Street.

ROD: I see—walk down Birch Street, turn right at the traffic lights into Oak Street and it's at the end of Oak Street on the right.

MAN: That's it. You can't miss it. It's Midland Bank.

ROD: Fine. Thank you very much.

MAN: You're welcome.

Why is Rod in Portland? *He is there* ....

Why did he want a bank? *Because* .... *for the weekend.*

Where did he park his car? .... *station.*

Where is the nearest bank? .... *Street.*

What's the name of the bank? .... *Bank.*

* * *

How do you get to the bank on Oak Street? *You* .... *Birch Street as far as the* .... *Then you* .... *into Oak Street. The bank* .... *Oak Street and Poplar Street.*

 Ask for and give directions

Walk down Birch Street as far as Oak Street.
Turn left/right into Oak Street.
Cross over Poplar Street.

The bank is $\left\{ \begin{array}{l} \text{half way down} \\ \text{at the end of} \\ \text{at the beginning of} \end{array} \right\}$ the street on the left/right.

It's $\left\{ \begin{array}{l} \text{next to/opposite the pub.} \\ \text{between the pub and the chemist.} \end{array} \right.$

1. **Work in pairs. Ask for and give directions in Portland. Start from the *bus station* each time. Like this:**

   Excuse me, is there a .... near here?

   Yes, $\left\{ \begin{array}{l} \text{the nearest one's} \\ \text{there's one} \end{array} \right\}$ in .... Street.

   How do I get to .... Street?

   You ....

   I see, you ....

   That's right.

   Thanks very much.

   You're welcome.

2. **Draw a sketch map of your local area and mark some of the places and streets. Work in pairs. Ask for and give directions to some of these places. Start from a railway or bus station.**

Oral Exercises

1. **Ask about facilities**

   You need a post office.
   Excuse me. Is there a post office near here?

   You need a bank.
   Excuse me. Is there a bank near here?

   You need a post office.
   You need a bank.
   You need a launderette.
   You want to see a film.
   You want to eat out.
   You want to change some travellers' cheques.

2. **Talk about facilities**

   Is there a library near here?
   Yes. There's a very good library over there.

   Is there a restaurant near here?
   Yes. There's a very good restaurant over there.

   Is there a library near here?
   Is there a restaurant near here?
   Is there a pub near here?
   Is there a hairdresser's near here?
   Is there a chemist's near here?
   Is there a Chinese restaurant near here?

3. **Answer questions about facilities**
   Look at the map of Portland on page 25.
   You are at the bus station in Birch Street.

   Is there a bank near here?
   Well, there isn't a bank in this street, but there's one in Oak Street. (And there's one in Elm Street.)
   Thanks.

   Is there a pub near here?
   Well, there isn't a pub in this street, but there's one in Poplar Street. (And there's one in Oak Street.)
   Thanks.

   Is there a bank near here?
   Is there a pub near here?
   Is there a launderette near here?
   Is there a hairdresser's near here?
   Is there a hamburger restaurant near here?
   Is there a cinema near here?
   Is there a Chinese restaurant near here?

4. **Talk about facilities**
   You are in Sutton.

   I'm looking for a hairdresser's.
   Well, there aren't any hairdressers here.

   I'm looking for a cinema.
   Well, there aren't any cinemas here.

   I'm looking for a hairdresser's.
   I'm looking for a cinema.
   I'm looking for a library.
   I'm looking for a park.
   I'm looking for a swimming pool.
   I'm looking for a playground.

5. **Ask for directions**

   You want to know the way to the supermarket.
   Excuse me. How do I get to the supermarket?

   You want to know the way to the swimming pool.
   Excuse me. How do I get to the swimming pool?

   You want to know the way to the supermarket.
   You want to know the way to the swimming pool.
   You want to know the way to the bus station.
   You want to know the way to the ABC cinema.
   You want to know the way to the post office.

6. **Repeat directions**

   You turn right and then left.
   I see. I turn right and then left.

   You walk down this road and then you turn right.
   I see. I walk down this road and then I turn right.

   You turn right and then left.
   You walk down this road and then you turn right.
   You cross over this road and take the first on your left.
   You take the second right and then right again.
   You turn left, then right and then left again.
   You take the third on the left and then cross over the square.

EXTENSION

TRANSPORT

SPORTS

CULTURAL

ENTERTAINMENT

← Railway Station

Stadium

LIBRARY ←

DISCOS

Underground

Swimming Pool

Restaurants ►

CINEMAS

TENNIS COURTS

OPERA HOUSE

CAFES

BUS STATION

FOOTBALL GROUND

THEATRE

Airport ↑

nightclubs

1. **Find the 'odd' words and complete the chart correctly.**

2. Read the article about Portland and Sutton again on page 27. Make notes about the article, like this:

	PORTLAND	SUTTON	YOUR TOWN
Description:	new, modern well-planned	post-war badly-planned	
Situation:			
Population:			
Facilities—			
essential:			
cultural:			
entertainment:			
sports:			

Now make similar notes about *your own* town.

3. Write a short description of your town and its facilities. Use the article as a model and your notes to help you. Try to link some of your sentences with *as well as* and *except for*.

4. Listen to Judith Hartley talking about the town she lives in. Note down the facilities she talks about.

Judith talks about the following facilities:
railway station
....
....
....

5. Listen to the telephone information about walks in central London. As you listen, trace with a pencil the directions on the map.

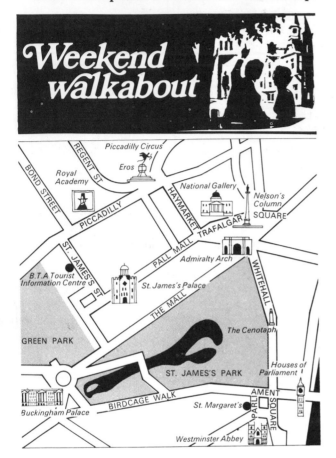

6. Barbara Cooper invited a friend to come and stay for the weekend.

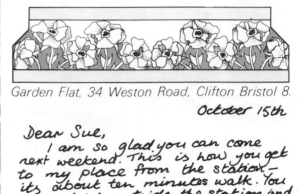

Garden Flat, 34 Weston Road, Clifton Bristol 8.

October 15th

Dear Sue,

I am so glad you can come next weekend. This is how you get to my place from the station — its about ten minutes walk. You turn right outside the station and walk down Station Road. Cross over Hatton Road and then turn left into Weston Road. It's the second house on the right — the one with the white door.

Or you can take the 33 bus from the station and get off at the corner of Weston Road. It's only two stops from the station.

See you about 2.30 p.m.

Love, Barbara.

P.S. My mother gave me this notepaper!

Write a similar letter to a friend. Describe how to get to your house from the nearest bus, railway or underground station.

CHECK

Now you can

1. Ask about facilities	Is there a bank near here? Are there any good restaurants near here?
2. Talk about facilities	There's a bank on Oak Street. There are two. There's one on Oak Street and one on Elm Street.
3. Ask for directions	How do I get to Oak Street? How do I get to the cinema?
4. Give directions	Walk down Elm Street as far as the traffic lights. Turn left into Poplar Street. The cinema is on your left.
5. Thank and respond to thanks	Thank you very much. You're welcome.

Grammar

There	is a pub	in Oak Street.
	are two banks	

There's no cinema There are no cinemas There aren't any cinemas	in Sutton.

Is Are	there	a chemist any restaurants	here?

Yes, No,	there	is. are. isn't. aren't.

at the	beginning end	of the street.
on the corner		

As well as Except for	a cinema,	there is a pub. there are two banks.
		there is no other form of entertainment. there aren't any entertainment facilities.

Words and phrases

launderette	playground	traffic lights	at the end of	plan
library	population	bus stop	half way down	park
chemist	thousand	stranger	between	cross over
hairdresser	service			get off
disco	entertainment	essential	As well as	turn
travel agency	facility	few	Except for	
night club	transport	near(est)	not even	
museum	corner	right	on business	
football ground	square	left	You're welcome	

UNIT 5

A place of my own

When Rod first started his job in Weston, he stayed in a small hostel. The hostel only served breakfast, so Rod had lunch in the canteen at work. When he finished work, he usually went to a cheap restaurant for his evening meal.

He didn't enjoy living in the hostel very much, so he decided to find a flat to rent. He soon found one just outside Bristol. It was quite a big flat on the top floor of a house owned by Joan and Norman Ingrams. Because the rent was quite high, and there were two bedrooms, Rod decided to find someone to share the flat with him. One morning he put an advertisement in the local newsagent's window.

The same day, a young student called Paul Blake went to the newsagent to buy a paper. When he saw the advertisement, he telephoned Rod immediately and asked permission to come and see the flat.

Where did Rod stay when he first started at Weston? *In a ....*

What meals did he have there? *He only had ....*

Where did he have his other meals? *He had .... at the .... and he went to a .... for his ....*

Why did he decide to find a flat? *Because he .... in the .... very much.*

Where was the flat situated? *......... Bristol.*

Who owned it?

Was the flat part of their house? *Yes, it was .... of their house.*

Why did Rod decide to find someone to share it?

How did he find someone? *He put .... in the ....*

Why did Paul Blake go to the newsagent's? *To .... a ....*

What did he do when he saw the advertisement? *He .... immediately.*

He saw the advertisement. Then he telephoned Rod immediately.
=
When he saw the advertisement, he telephoned Rod.

A. Link these sentences using *'when'*.

He got home. Then he telephoned Rod.

He found his address book. Then he wrote Rod's name in it.

He telephoned Rod. Then he asked permission to come and see the flat.

* * *

Why did Rod decide to rent a flat of his own?

What did he do?

What happened?

Try to link your answers with *when, so, because, and, but* or *then.*

FLAT TO SHARE

Big flat, just outside
Bristol. £12 a week.
Own bedroom. Share
kitchen, bathroom.
Telephone Rod, 367594

**B. Listen to the telephone conversation be-
tween Paul Blake and Rod Nelson. As you
listen, mark TRUE or FALSE against the
following statements.**

	TRUE	FALSE
1. Paul is a friend of Rod's.		
2. Rod's flat has one bedroom.		
3. Not all the rooms are on the same floor.		
4. Paul must pay half the rent.		
5. Paul is a student at a Polytechnic.		
6. He studies electrical engineering and maths.		
7. He decided to go and see the flat on Saturday afternoon.		
8. The address is 57 London Road.		
9. Paul will need two keys if he takes the flat.		
10. The Ingrams do not live in the house.		

SET 1   Ask for, give and refuse permission

(formally)	May I come and see the flat?	Yes, of course. Yes, certainly.
(informally)	Can I come and see you?	Yes, sure. Yes, do.

1. **Work in pairs. Ask for permission to do these things:**

open the door	close the door
borrow your book	turn on the light
use your telephone	turn on the television

Ask for and give permission, first formally, then informally.

May I use your phone?	Well, actually, I'm expecting a phone call myself.
Can I use your phone?	Sorry, but I'm expecting a call.

---

2. **Work in pairs. Ask for and refuse permission, first formally, then informally. Use a different reason each time.**

May I . . . ?	Well, actually . . .
Can I . . . ?	Sorry, but . . .
come and see you this evening	I've got guests for supper. I want to go to bed early.
smoke	this is a no-smoking room. I feel sick when people smoke.
telephone you at work	I haven't got a phone. my boss doesn't like it.
open the window	it's very noisy when it's open. I've got an awful cold.
borrow your car	there's no petrol in it. I need it myself.
play your new Abba record	I lent it to my sister. the record player is broken.

3. **What do you say to:**

a friend when the room is hot and you've got a headache?

a stranger when you need to make a phone call in his house?

a stranger when you want to look at his newspaper on the train?

a friend when you want to talk to him/her alone?

Act these situations with a partner.

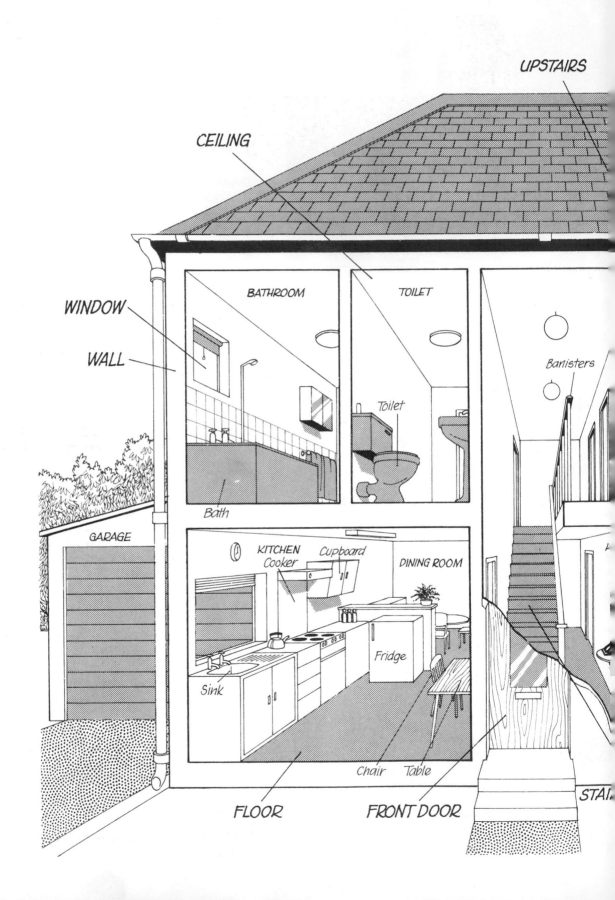

UPSTAIRS

CEILING

WINDOW

WALL

BATHROOM

TOILET

Banisters

Toilet

Bath

GARAGE

KITCHEN
Cooker

Cupboard

DINING ROOM

Fridge

Sink

Chair

Table

FLOOR

FRONT DOOR

STAI

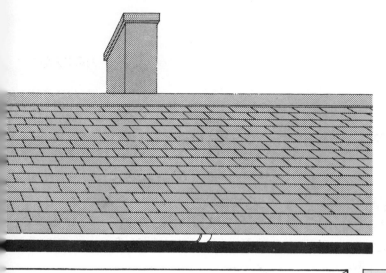

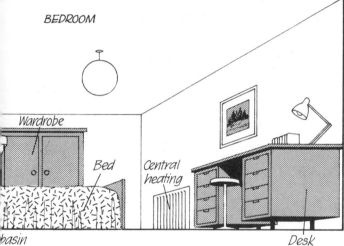

BEDROOM

Wardrobe

Bed

Central heating

Desk

basin

rtain

hair

SITTING ROOM

Record player

Lamp

Television

fa

Carpet

Book case

DOWNSTAIRS

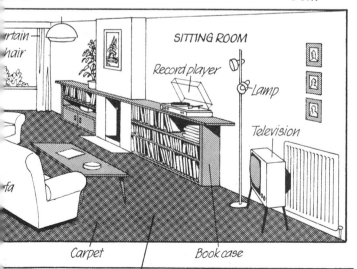

SET 2 — Describe houses and furniture

1. **How many rooms are there in this house? Name them like this:**
   There are .... rooms.
   There's a ...., a .... *etc.*

2. **What furniture and fittings are there in the bedroom/kitchen/sittingroom? Answer like this:**
   In the bedroom, there's a ....

3. *Either* **write down the names of the *rooms* in your house or flat and what *furniture* and *fittings* there are in each of them,**
   or **draw a plan of your house or flat and label all the *rooms* and *furniture*.**

4. **Write a short description of the house like this:**
   This is quite a big house. There is an upstairs and a downstairs.
   Downstairs there is a .... (*name rooms*) and upstairs there's a .... and a .... (*name rooms*). In the bedroom upstairs there's a .... (*name furniture*). Downstairs in the sittingroom there's a .... (*name furniture*). In the kitchen there's a ....(*name furniture etc.*).

5. **Now write a short description of your house/flat.**

SIZE	large	small	high	low			
TEXTURE	hard	soft	heavy	light			
COLOUR	dark	light	red	blue	green	yellow	purple
	black	white	grey	brown	orange	pink	beige

PATTERN	plain	flowery	striped	checked
SHAPE	round	oval	square	rectangular
MATERIAL*	wood	metal	plastic	leather	glass	material

*Like this: The table is made of wood/glass.
The chair is made of plastic/leather/a soft material.

---

6. **Game: What is it?**

   Work in groups. One person chooses something in the room. The others must guess what it is. Ask questions like:

   Is it round? Is it soft? Is it large? Is it red?
   Is it in the corner? Is it on the floor? *etc.*

7. **Think of your bedroom or sittingroom at home. Work in pairs.**
   Ask and answer questions like:

What about the carpet?
What furniture is there in the room?
(Describe it—size, colour, shape, material)
What colour are the walls?
What are the curtains like? What colour are they?

8. **Write a paragraph describing the room and the furniture in it.**
   Say if you like the room. Give reasons.

Oral Exercises

1. Ask for permission informally and formally

You are in a friend's house. You want to use the phone.
Can I use the phone?
Yes, do.

You are at your boss's house. You want to use the bathroom.
May I use the bathroom?
Yes, of course.

You are at a friend's house. You want to use the phone.
You are at your boss's house. You want to use the bathroom.
You are at your parents' house. You want to watch television.
You are on a train. You want to borrow a newspaper from another passenger.
You are at a friend's house. You want to make a cup of tea.
You are in a crowded cafe; there is only one seat next to an old lady. You want to sit down.
You are at a friend's house. You want to play some records.

**2.* Refuse permission formally and informally
Look at page 34. Choose the best reason for refusing permission.**

May I come and see you this evening?
Well, actually, (I've got guests for supper).

Can I smoke here?
Sorry, but (I feel sick when people smoke).

May I come and see you this evening?
Can I smoke here?
Can I telephone you at work?
May I open the window?
Can I borrow your car?
May I play your new Abba record?

3. Describe things

What shape is an apple?
Round.
What colours are the British flag?
Red, white and blue.
What shape is an apple?
What colours are the British flag?
What's a record made of?
What shape is a football field?
What's a football made of?
What's a window made of?
What shape is a chessboard?
What colours are your country's flag?

**4. Comment on colours
A friend is describing her new house to you.**

What colour's the house?
Green and white.
Mmm. A green and white house. That sounds nice.

What colour's the kitchen?
Yellow.
Mmm. A yellow kitchen. That sounds nice.

What colour's the house? (Green and white.)
What colour's the kitchen? (Yellow.)
What colour are the kitchen curtains? (Green and white checked.)
What about the sittingroom? What colour are the walls? (Dark blue.)
And the carpet? (Plain white.)
What about the curtains? (Pink and white striped.)

**5. Ask about furniture
You are going to rent a house for a month. You ring the house agent to see what there is in the house. Look at the plan on page 35.**

Ask about a sofa.
Is there a sofa in the sittingroom?
Oh, yes.

Ask about a fridge.
Is there a fridge in the kitchen?
Of course.

Ask about:

1. a sofa 2. a fridge 3. a wardrobe 4. a cooker
5. a washbasin 6. a record player

EXTENSION

1. Those difficult requests

I was on a train the other day, in an empty compartment, and I wanted to read the last chapter of my Agatha Christie book. Then the door opened and a mother with a baby and two small children asked me: 'May we sit here?' At first I wanted to say: 'Well, actually, I'm reading an exciting book and I'd like to finish it. Could you find another compartment?'

But of course I said, 'Yes, certainly.' I still have not finished that last chapter. Unfortunately, I find it very difficult to say 'No' to those magic words 'May I . . . ' or 'Do you mind if I . . . '

Of course, people usually ask permission to do quite harmless things, like use the telephone, turn the light on, open the window and things like that. But then there are some ridiculous requests. Some people even ask if they may use the lavatory, wash their hands and take their coats off. (On the other hand, very few smokers will bother to ask permission to smoke!)

But what about those difficult requests like: 'Can I use your phone? I promised to ring my mother in Edinburgh.' when you live in Bristol. Or 'Do you mind if I come round for a cup of coffee?' when you are busy doing the housework. Or 'Is it all right if I bring the children to the party? They're very good really.' The trouble is, I just don't have the nerve to refuse. Well, do you?

a) What happened on the train?
   The author was in an empty ....

b) Find 4 ways of *asking permission*. Write them down.

c) What examples does the author give of:
   i harmless requests for permission.
   ii ridiculous requests.
   iii difficult requests.

d) Do people in your country ask permission to smoke, use the phone, pour themselves a drink in a friend's house? What other things do people ask permission to do?

2. Listen to these two people describing their bedrooms. Make notes as you listen.

	Furniture etc.	Description (size/colour etc)
Kevin		
Sally		

3. Work in groups. You decide to turn your classroom into a student common room. What do you want it to look like?

Discuss what furniture you would like.
Do you want curtains and a carpet? If so, what colour/material?
What about the walls and ceiling? Are they all right or do you want a different colour?
Draw a plan of the room as you would like to see it.
Label the furniture and show the other groups.
Use words like:

I'd like to have . . .
Why don't we get a . . . ?
What about } buying { a . . . ?
How about } buying { some . . . ?
Yes, that's a good idea.
No, I'm not so keen on . . . .

CHECK

Now you can:

1. Ask for permission formally and informally	May I use your phone? Can I use your phone?
2. Give permission formally and informally	Yes, of course. Yes, certainly. Yes, sure. Yes, do.
3. Refuse permission formally and informally	Well, actually I'm . . . Sorry, but I'm . . .
4. Describe your house and furniture	There are three rooms upstairs and four rooms downstairs. In my bedroom there is a wardrobe and a desk. The curtains are red and white checked.
5. Link sentences with 'when'	He phoned *when* he saw the advertisement.

Grammar

May Can	I	use your phone? close the door?

When he saw it, he	went home. telephoned Rod. told his parents.

It's made of	plastic. leather. glass. a soft material.

A soft light blue A large leather An old, black and white checked A round glass	carpet. chair. sofa. table.

Words and phrases

newsagent	sink	wood	blue	exciting
top	central heating	metal	green	noisy
half	cooker	plastic	yellow	
rent	fridge	leather	grey	serve
key	armchair	material	brown	share
guest	sofa		orange	borrow
boss	bookcase	large	pink	lend
hand	cupboard	high	purple	use
coat	dressing table	low	beige	wash
wall	chair	hard	plain	turn on
floor	desk	soft	flowery	
ceiling	lamp	heavy	striped	Sure!
wardrobe	curtain	light (weight)	checked	Do!
washbasin	carpet	dark	round	Certainly!
		light (colour)	oval	immediately
			square	
			rectangular	

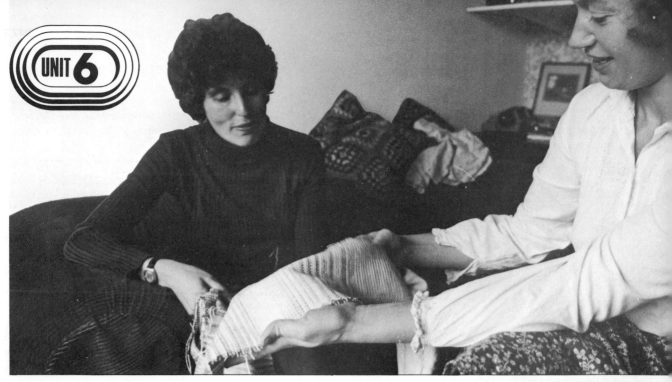

Joan Ingram calls in to see her neighbour Pat one Saturday morning.

JOAN: Hello, Pat. Are you busy?
PAT: Oh, hello, Joan. Come in. No, I'm not busy.
JOAN: How do you feel now? How's your cold?
PAT: Oh, much better, thanks.
JOAN: Oh, good. I *am* glad. Look, would you like to come into town with me this morning and buy some curtain material?
PAT: Yes, I'd love to. What about going to Barker's? They usually have good materials.
JOAN: Mmm. I'm not so keen on Barker's. It's so expensive there. But there's a good shop which sells materials in Patton Street. It's called Bailey's.
PAT: Bailey's? I don't know it. How do you get to it?
JOAN: Well, you walk down Broad Street and turn right at the second traffic lights, and then you're in Patton Street. Bailey's is about half way down on the left.

Later that morning in Bailey's.

GIRL: Can I help you? Or are you just looking?
JOAN: Well, yes, actually. I'm looking for some plain curtain material. Dark blue, I think.
GIRL: Well, the plain materials are over there. Why don't you have a look? I'll be back in a minute.
JOAN: Thank you. What do you think of this, Pat?
PAT: Mmm. It's all right. But it isn't dark blue.
JOAN: No, and it's rather expensive.
GIRL: Have you found anything you like?
JOAN: Er . . . I'm not sure. May I take a sample of this material?
GIRL: Yes, of course. Here you are.
JOAN: Thank you very much.
GIRL: You're welcome.
JOAN: *(to Pat)* Let's go to Barker's after all!

consolidation

1. In the dialogue, find examples of how to:

greet someone informally
ask about someone's health
answer about one's health
invite someone to do something
accept an invitation
make a suggestion
disagree
talk about a facility/service
ask for directions
give directions
describe what one is looking for
ask for an opinion
express an opinion
ask for permission to do something
give permission
thank someone
respond to thanks

2. Practise the dialogue in pairs.

3. Roleplay

You call on a friend and invite him/her to come with you to buy a dress or a pair of trousers/jeans.
Discuss where to go and how to get there.
In the shop, ask your friend's opinion about the clothes you look at.
Ask permission of the girl/man in the shop to try the clothes on.
If you like the clothes, ask the girl/man if you can have them.
If you do not like the clothes, suggest going to another shop.

4. Asking permission

Ruth, a good friend of Barbara's, comes to see her one day after work. Ruth usually does what she wants, but she always asks permission first.
Complete the conversation between Ruth and Barbara, using the following phrases:

Can I ...?   Yes, sure!
                  Yes, do!
                  Sorry, but ...

BARBARA: Ruth! How nice to see you! Come in!
RUTH: Thanks. Phew! I'm tired. ....?
BARBARA: .... That's the comfortable chair over there.
RUTH: Great! Thanks. Oh, what's the time, by the way?
BARBARA: Quarter past six.
RUTH: Oh, dear. Is it? I must ring Terry. ....?
BARBARA: .... It's in the hall.
RUTH: Thanks.
(She goes to ring Terry. A few minutes later she comes back.)
        Terry sends his regards.
BARBARA: Oh, thanks.
RUTH: What's that book, Barbara?
BARBARA: Oh, sorry. It's just the last chapter. It's the new Alistair Maclean novel. It's very exciting.
RUTH: ....?
BARBARA: .... I promised to lend it to Rod.
RUTH: Oh, that's all right. Barbara, I would love a cup of coffee. ....?
BARBARA: .... You know where the kitchen is. Why don't you make me one too?
RUTH: OK. And then you must tell me all about Rod . . .

5. Complete the conversational exchanges.

1. A: ....?
   No, I'm not.
   A: ....?
   B: From Belgium.

2. A: ....?
   B: No, not much. My husband does most of the cooking.

3. A: ....?
   B: It's all right. But London is like most big cities—noisy, dirty and depressing if you don't know anyone.

4. A: Shall we go to the Flamingo Club this evening?
   B: ....
   A: Well, *what* shall we do then? I'm bored.
   B: ....
   A: But there's nothing good on at the cinema this week.

5. A: ....?
   B: I've got a headache, that's all.
   A: ....

6. A: ....?
   B: Oh, much better, thank you.
   A: ....

7. A: ....?
   B: No, not very well, I'm afraid. You see, I never sleep well in a strange bed.

8. A: ....?
   B: Yes, we did, thanks. A lovely weekend.
   A: ....?
   B: We went to see some friends in Exeter.

9. A: ....?
   B: Yes, there's one on Broad Street. It sells all sorts of records—classical, pop, rock, jazz—everything.

10. A: ....?
    B: You take the 67 bus to the corner of Broad Street and then walk. The library is halfway down the street on the left hand side.

11. A: ....?
    B: Yes, of course. I think the News starts in five minutes. I'm afraid we only have black and white.

12. A: May I use your phone for a minute?
    B: .... I'm expecting a call from France any minute now.

6. Guess the job

Listen to this young man talking about his job.

He will give you five clues. If you can guess his job after the first clue, write it down. If you are right, you score five points. If you can't guess, listen to the next clue. If you guess right, you score four points. And so on.

If you guess the job after five clues, you only get one point.

Clue 1 (5 points): ....
    2 (4 points): ....
    3 (3 points): ....
    4 (2 points): ....
    5 (1 point): ....

7. A telephone message

Listen to a telephone conversation at Weston Aeronautics. Lynne Thomas, a secretary, answers the phone and takes a message. Listen and write down the message.

```
TELEPHONE MESSAGE
To:
From:
Message:
```

8. Roleplay

Work in pairs. Your partner is a visitor to your home town. You are a reporter for a local newspaper. You are going to write an article about foreigners' opinions about your home town.

Interview your partner.
Find out:

1. his/her name and nationality.
2. why he/she is visiting your home town.
3. his/her opinions about it.
4. what he/she likes doing in his/her spare time.

Then

1. Suggest a meeting with him/her for lunch later in the week.
2. Name a place to meet.
3. Give directions to get there.

9. Recent holidays

Look at the chart where people live in
Unit 1 on page 3.
Try to remember the last holiday you had.
Use the words in the chart to describe:

1. where you went
2. what part of the country it was
3. what the countryside/surroundings were like
4. where you stayed
5. what you did while you were there.

Work in pairs. Tell your partner about
your holiday.

10. American visitors

Robert Selinker and his wife, Louise, with
their children, Barbi aged 15 and Matt
aged 19, are visiting your country for a
week next summer. This is their first visit
to your country.
Both Robert and Louise like sightseeing
and eating food from other countries.
Louise is interested in photography, too.
Barbi likes dancing and Matt likes sport.
Plan an interesting holiday in your country
for the Selinker family. Work in groups.
Make suggestions like this:

Why don't we { take them to …?
{ show them …?
Let's take Matt/Barbi to ….
What about visiting …?
How about going to …?

11. Two games

A) Remember! Remember!
You have 5 minutes.
Write down as many
COLOURS,
PIECES OF FURNITURE,
SHAPES
and MATERIALS as you can remember!

B) Twenty Questions
One person thinks of a piece of furniture
or object. The others must try to guess
what it is in less than 20 questions.
They can only ask questions with a
'Yes' or 'No' answer. Like this:
Is it red?
Is it made of plastic?
etc.

UNIT 7

GUESTS FOR SUPPER

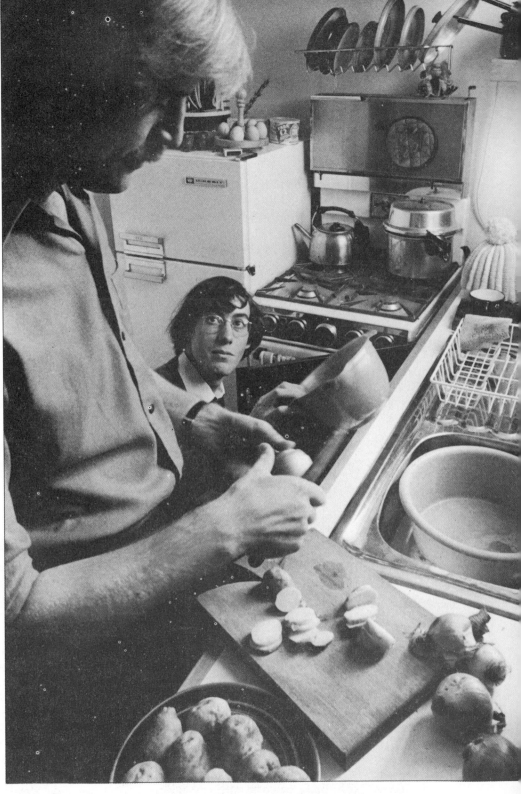

Rod and Paul have invited Barbara and Sue, Paul's girlfriend, to supper. They are in the kitchen getting supper ready.

PAUL: What have we got in the fridge, Rod?
ROD: Nothing much. We've got some ham, eggs, cheese . . .
PAUL: Have we got any potatoes?
ROD: I think so. Yes, we have. And we've got some onions too.

PAUL: Well, why don't we have some ham and a Danish potato salad? I copied down the recipe from the radio yesterday.

(a few minutes later)

ROD: Let's see now. Cut the potatoes into small cubes . . .

PAUL: Yes, but don't cut them yet. Wait until they're cool. Where's the big red plastic bowl?

ROD: On the bottom shelf in the cupboard under the sink.

PAUL: What's Barbara like, by the way?

ROD: Barbara? Well, she's in her mid-twenties. She's very lively. She's got a good sense of humour. I think you'll like her. What about Sue?

PAUL: Oh, Sue's very easy-going and friendly.

ROD: Could you get me the mayonnaise from the cupboard?

PAUL: Yes, sure. Which cupboard is it in?

ROD: It's in the small one beside the cooker.

PAUL: There's no mayonnaise here.

ROD: Oh, isn't there? Oh, no! The recipe says parsley and lemon. I know we haven't got . . .

(Doorbell rings)

They're here!

BARBARA: Hello! Here we are! You're Paul, are you? What's the matter? You both look miserable!

PAUL: We're making a potato salad and . . .

ROD: . . . we haven't got any mayonnaise, or parsley or lemon!

SUE: Well, that's all right. I'm on a diet.

BARBARA: And I *hate* potato salad. So that's fine. Here, I've got some wine. Let's have a glass now!

Who are Rod and Paul's guests?

What does Paul suggest they have for supper?

Where did he get the recipe from?

Why isn't Sue so keen on potato salad?

Does Barbara like it?

* * *

What have Rod and Paul got in their fridge?

Have they got any potatoes?

Have they got any mayonnaise?

What else haven't they got?

Where is the big red plastic bowl?

Where does Rod say the mayonnaise is?

What is Barbara like?

What is Sue like?

Do you agree?

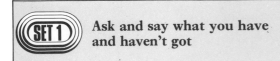

SET 1   Ask and say what you have and haven't got

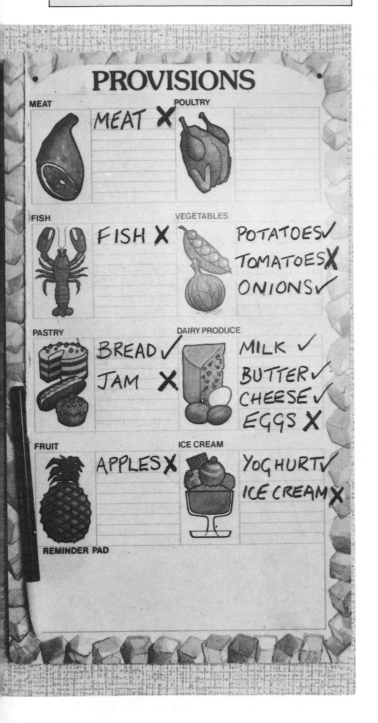

Have we got any milk? Yes, we've got lots of milk.
Have we got any meat? No, we haven't.

1. **Work in pairs. Look at the kitchen list. Ask and answer like this:**

   Have we got any ....?
   Yes, we've got lots of .... *or*
   No, we haven't.

Have we got anything
  to eat?   We've got some bread.
What else have we got?   We've got some cheese.
What else?

2. **Look at the list again. Ask and answer like this:**

   Have we got anything to eat?
   We've got some ....
   What else have we got? *or* What else?
   We've got some ....

What have we got? What about tomatoes?
No, we haven't got any tomatoes.
What about meat?
No, we haven't got any meat.

3. **Look at the things on the list marked with an X. Ask and answer like this:**

   What have we got? What about ....?
   No, we haven't got any ....
   What about ....?
   No, we haven't got any ....

4. **Look at the list and say what you have or haven't got at home. Choose only a few things from the list. Like this:**

   I've got some milk, butter and cheese, but I haven't got any fish or meat.

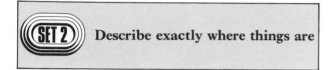

SET 2   **Describe exactly where things are**

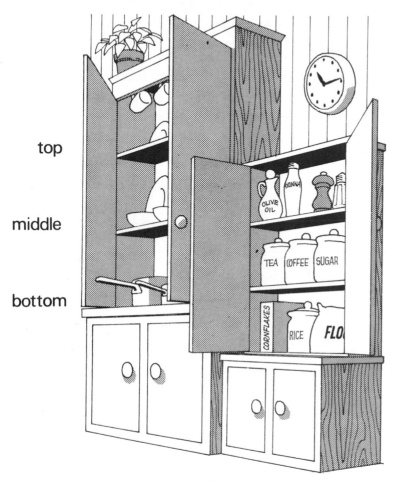

top

middle

bottom

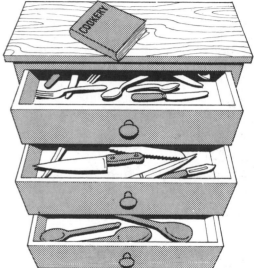

mayonnaise	salt	cups and saucers	
olive oil	pepper	plates	
coffee	flour	bowls	
tea	cornflakes	saucepans	
sugar	rice		

knives, forks and spoons
kitchen knives
wooden spoons

Where's the mayonnaise?	In the cupboard.
Which one?	The small one.
Where exactly?	On the top shelf.

Where are the knives and forks?	In the drawer beside the cooker.
Which drawer?	The top one.

1. **Work in pairs. Look at the cupboards. Ask and say exactly where things are.**

2. **Work in pairs. Look at the drawers. Ask and say exactly where the knives, etc. are.**

SET 3   **Ask people to do things**

Could you get me the mayonnaise from the cupboard?
Yes, sure.

1. **Work in pairs. Look at the kitchen list on page 47. Ask your partner to get you those things marked with an X. Like this:**

I'm going to the supermarket. Do you want anything?
Oh, yes. Could you get me some milk, please?
Yes, sure. Do you want anything else?
Yes. Could you get me some .... as well?

YOU	YOUR PARTNER
1 like salad and fruit.	is going to the greengrocer's.
2 would like some sweets.	is going to the sweetshop.
3 want a newspaper.	is going to the newsagent's.
4 have a bad cold.	is going to the chemist's.
5 are thirsty.	is going to the kitchen.

2. **Look at these situations. Make a list of the things you want. Like this:**

Salad and fruit: tomatoes, lettuce
                       oranges, apples

Then ask your partner to get you things. Like this:

I'm going to the greengrocer's. Do you want anything?
Oh, yes. Could you get me some tomatoes and some lettuce, please? And could you get me some oranges and apples as well?

A holiday in the sun? Lovely! But be careful!

JOSE, a Spanish hotel owner on the Costa Brava, says: 'Tourists! Sometimes they are stupid! They go straight to the beach on their first day and lie in the sun for hours. Then they have to stay in bed for a week! It is better to sunbathe for just half an hour the first day.

'And they go to the beach in the middle of the day, when the sun is very hot. The morning is better—or late afternoon.

'And why do people swim immediately after a heavy lunch? This can be dangerous. It is better to wait for an hour or two.

'Another thing—people often take lots of money with them on to the beach. This is stupid. There are lots of thieves about, unfortunately. It is better to have travellers' cheques.

'It is also dangerous to carry passports and tickets on you. Much better to lock them in your hotel room.

'Of course, it's common sense. But tourists leave their common sense at home when they go on holiday.'

SET 4 Give instructions and advice

1. Read the article and make a list of instructions for the tourist abroad. Like this:

Don't lie in the sun for hours on your first day. Sunbathe for just half an hour.
Don't go to .... Go in the ....
Don't ....
....
....

2. Make up some instructions for tourists on holiday in your town/country.

Warning hints

Cash Do not carry a large amount of cash on your person. If it is stolen or lost it is not likely to be recovered. Carry only enough cash to meet your day-to-day expenses. If you are staying in a hotel hand any large sum of cash to the manager for safe keeping and obtain a receipt.

Travellers' cheques These should be in small denominations such as £5 and £10 to enable you to have sufficient money for your daily needs. Keep a note of the serial numbers in case of loss as you will be able to give this information to your bank's agents if you have to report a loss.

Wallets Carry your wallet in an inside pocket, never in your back trouser pocket. If you take off your jacket transfer your wallet to your trouser pocket.

Handbags Never leave your handbag unattended even for short periods. Always take it with you.

Hand luggage Do not leave hand luggage including your briefcase unattended on railway platforms, waiting rooms, luggage racks or anywhere else. Valuables such as a camera, radio, portable typewriter should be carried and you should keep a note of the serial number.

Documents Special care should be taken of your passport, air tickets and other personal documents.

Self-service shops

Always use the baskets in self-service shops or supermarkets if these are provided for you to place the goods you intend to purchase. Always pay for goods before leaving the shop. Failure to do so is very likely to lead to accusation and police prosecution for shoplifting.

o's & Dont's

carry your passport, your money and Travel
ques in a safe place – not just flung into a
ch bag, or all in one pocket or wallet.

check rates of exchange when you cash your
eques – a shopkeeper or hotelier may,
gitimately, lower the rate a little; make sure it is
nly a little!

Do fill in the detachable slip you will find in your
Travel Cheque book and keep this record of your
cheque numbers in a safe and separate place.

Don't countersign unless in the presence of the
person who gives value for the cheque.

Do keep some Travel Cheques or notes in reserve
for emergencies. **Don** ever put yourself in the
awful position of finding yourself abroad and flat
broke.

Do expect to be asked for some proof of identity
when encashing Travel Cheques: take your
passport with you.

Oral Exercises

1. Confirm that you've got things

Have you got any eggs?
Oh, yes, lots of eggs.

Have you got any butter?
Oh, yes, lots of butter.

Have you got any eggs?
Have you got any butter?
Have you got any onions?
Have you got any cheese?
Have you got any bread?
Have you got any potatoes?

2. Say what you have and haven't got
Look at the kitchen list on page 47.

Now, we need some onions and tomatoes.
Well, there are some onions, but we haven't got any tomatoes.

What about milk and eggs?
Well, there is some milk, but we haven't got any eggs.

Now, we need some onions and tomatoes.
What about milk and eggs?
Then we need butter and fish.
What about bread and meat?
Finally, we need yoghurt and apples.

3.* Ask what people have got
You are staying with a friend for the week-end. Think about what you would like to eat and ask your friend if he has got any.

Now what would you like for breakfast?
Have you got any (eggs)?

Yes, sure. And what would you like with your coffee?
Have you got any (chocolate biscuits)?

Now what would you like for breakfast?
Yes, sure. And what would you like with your coffee?
No, I haven't. I'll get some for you. What about lunch? What would you like?
I think so. I'll have a look in the fridge. What would you like to drink with your lunch?
Yes, I have. And what would you like to have for tea?
No, I haven't. I'll go to the supermarket. Finally, there's supper. Is there anything special you would like?

4. Say where things are exactly
Look at the cupboards and drawers on page 48.

Where's the mayonnaise?
In the small cupboard on the top shelf.

Where are the kitchen knives?
In the middle drawer.

Where's the mayonnaise?
Where are the kitchen knives?
Where's the coffee?
Where are the cups and saucers?
Where's the flour?
Where are the bowls?

5. Ask people to do things in different ways
Repeat these sentences.

Give me a lift to the station, Rod.
Can you give me a lift to the station, Rod?
Could you give me a lift to the station, Rod?
Could you give me a lift to the station, please, Rod?
Could you possibly give me a lift to the station, please, Rod?

Which request is least polite? ....
Which request is most polite? ....

6. Give warnings
A friend is planning a trip. You don't think his plans are very sensible.

I'm going in the middle of August.
Oh, don't go in the middle of August. That's not a good idea.

Well, I don't think so. I'm driving too.
Oh, don't drive. That's not a good idea.

I'm going in the middle of August.
I'm driving too.
And I'm leaving on Friday evening.
I'm taking the children too.
I'm driving all night.
I think I'll go through Central London.

EXTENSION

 1. Last summer, the Ingrams exchanged houses with some friends who live on the south coast of England. Joan Ingram left a note to say where to find things.

Dear Anne,

Just a short note to say where things are in the house. The sheets and towels are in the cupboard at the top of the stairs. Extra blankets are in the yellow wardrobe in the small bedroom.

The vacuum cleaner is in the cupboard under the stairs. There's a spare front door key on the shelf above the sink in the kitchen.

One more thing. Could you feed the cats? * Don't feed them more than once a day as they're on a diet! Also could you give them some water in their bowl outside the back door every day? Don't give them milk — they don't like it!

Hope you have a good time.

Love,

Joan.

* The cat food is in the small cupboard under the sink in the kitchen.

Imagine someone is going to stay in your room/flat/house.
Write a note to say where things are.
Give any instructions you think are necessary.

2. Listen to these four short conversations. In each one, someone asks another person to do something.
The first conversation is complete; the other three have gaps. Write down the sentence that you think will fill the gap in each conversation. Like this:

Conversation 1: Could you give me a lift to the station?
Conversation 2:
Conversation 3:
Conversation 4:

DANISH POTATO SALAD

Ingredients (for 6 people):

1 kg. potatoes

2 large onions

2½ dl. mayonnaise

½ tbsp. fresh lemon juice

chopped parsley

salt and pepper

⑧ Sprinkle with parsley.

⑥ Fold in tablespoon of chopped parsley.

⑤ Mix ½ tablespoon of lemon juice with the seasoned mayonnaise.

② Peel and cook 1kg. of potatoes in salted boiling water. Leave to cool.

④ Finely chop onions.

⑨ Chill in fridge.

③ Cut potatoes into small cubes.

⑦ Mix potatoes and onions into mayonnaise.

① You need 1kg. potatoes, 2 large onions, mayonnaise, lemon juice, parsley, salt and pepper.

3. The instructions are in the wrong order. Listen to the instructions for making Danish Potato Salad on the tape and number the pictures in the correct order. Write 1 by the first step, 2 by the second step and so on. When the instructions are in the right order, write them out in full. Like this:

Instructions for making a Danish Potato Salad
First peel and cook ………
Next ………
Then ………

CHECK

Now you can:

1. Ask what people have got
Have you got any milk?
What have we got?

2. Say what you have got
We've got some cheese.
We haven't got any milk.
We've got lots of tomatoes.

3. Describe exactly where things are
It's in the small cupboard on the top shelf.
It's in the blue one.

4. Ask people and agree to do things
Could you get me the mayonnaise from the cupboard?
Yes, sure.

5. Give instructions
Don't take a lot of money with you.
Lock it up.

Grammar

I've He's She's We've You've They've	got	some lots of	milk.

Have / Has	you we they / he she	got any	coffee? / bread?

I We You They / He She	haven't / hasn't	got any	tea. wine. / lemon.

On the shelf in the cupboard	under above beside at the top of	the . . .

On In	the	top middle bottom	shelf. drawer.

Put all your money away. Don't put any money in the drawer. Don't take any money with you.

Could you	give get	me him her us them	a lift to the station, another cup of tea,	please?

Words and phrases

girlfriend
ham
onion
recipe
bowl
shelf
sense of humour
mayonnaise
lettuce
parsley
diet (on a . . .)

yoghurt
jam
olive oil
pepper
flour
sweets
rice
saucer
saucepan
knife
fork

spoon
drawer
thief
money
travellers' cheques
passport
sheet
towel
blanket
vacuum cleaner
sweetshop

lively
easy-going

copy
cut
lie
sunbathe
wait
carry
lock

in
on
under
above
beside
middle
bottom
mid (in her mid-twenties)
not at all
something
anything

'Could you answer the phone? I'm washing my hair.'
'Could you ring back later? We're having supper.'
'Could you phone back tomorrow morning? We're in the middle of painting the bathroom?'

Excuses

SET 1 Ask and talk about present actions

1. Work in pairs. Match the pictures with the actions. Ask and answer like this:

What's the boy in Picture 1 doing?
He's listening to records.
What are the people in Picture 2 doing?
They're entertaining friends.

Choose from these actions:

doing the housework
relaxing on the sofa
reading
feeding the baby
having a shower
painting the kitchen

putting the children to bed
washing her hair
making lunch
reading to the children
entertaining friends
listening to records

2. Look at the list. Choose *three* bad times for people to phone (when you're doing something). Like this:

It's a bad time to phone when I'm ………
    when ………
    ………

3. Work in pairs. Look at the list again and ask and answer like this:

Do you mind people phoning you when you're (washing your hair?)
Yes, definitely. *or*
No, not really. *or*
Sometimes. It depends.

Lynne, a secretary who works in the same office as Rod, has family problems. Rod invites her round to his flat one evening to talk about them.
He is expecting her to arrive soon. Suddenly the telephone rings. He goes to answer it.

BARBARA: Hello, Rod! Barbara here.
ROD: Oh. Oh, hello, Barbara.
BARBARA: Er . . . are you busy?
ROD: Well, yes, actually. I'm just having a shower.
BARBARA: Oh, sorry. I'll ring back later. OK?
ROD: Er . . . yes. Fine. Bye!

Are you busy?	Well, yes, actually. I'm just having a shower.
Am I ringing at a bad time?	No, I'm just watching TV, but that's all right.

4. Write down what the people are doing in the picture.

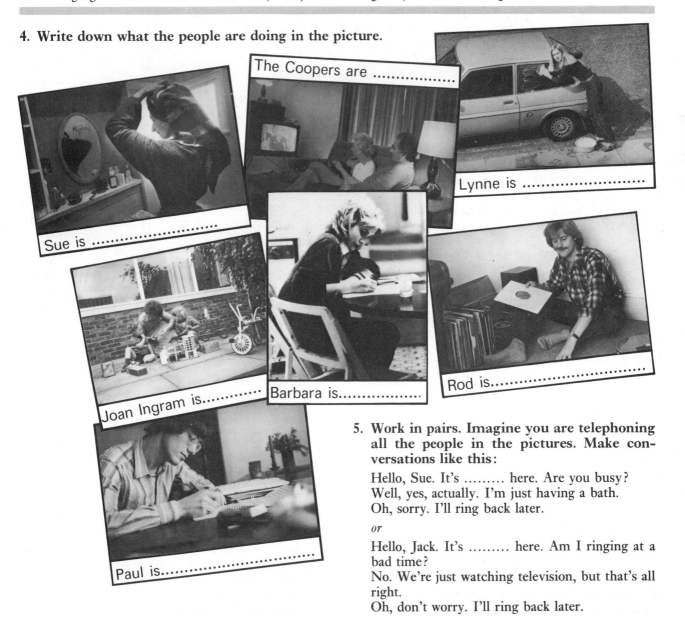

The Coopers are ....

Lynne is ....

Sue is ....

Joan Ingram is ....

Barbara is ....

Rod is ....

Paul is ....

5. Work in pairs. Imagine you are telephoning all the people in the pictures. Make conversations like this:

Hello, Sue. It's .... here. Are you busy?
Well, yes, actually. I'm just having a bath.
Oh, sorry. I'll ring back later.

or

Hello, Jack. It's .... here. Am I ringing at a bad time?
No. We're just watching television, but that's all right.
Oh, don't worry. I'll ring back later.

Barbara telephones Rod again half an hour later. Lynne is already there.

BARBARA: Rod? It's me, Barbara. Am I ringing at a bad time again?

ROD: No, no. That's all right. Is it something important?

BARBARA: No, not really. It's just . . . well, some American friends of mine are here for a few days and they wanted to go for a meal this evening. I thought maybe you'd like to come too.

ROD: Well, that does sound fun, but . . . er . . . I'm afraid, I've got a bad headache, to tell you the truth, and . . .

BARBARA: Oh, have you? I *am* sorry. Why don't you take a couple of aspirins and lie down for a bit? You'll be all right in half an hour.

ROD: Yes, I know, but it's not just the headache. I'm afraid I really ought to do my washing this evening and I've got to write home to my parents too.

BARBARA: Oh, well, shall we come round for a coffee later on instead?

ROD: Actùally, I'd like to go to bed early tonight for once.

BARBARA: Oh, all right. Some other time then.

ROD: Look, Barbara, I'll ring you at work some time tomorrow.

BARBARA: Don't you remember? I'm leaving for Italy tomorrow.

ROD: Oh, yes. Of course. So you are. I remember now.

BARBARA: Well, have a nice evening, Rod.

ROD: Wait a minute, Barbara. I'll ring you early tomorrow morning and . . .

BARBARA: It's OK, Rod. I understand—perfectly. See you around.

(click)

Is Rod alone in the flat when Barbara rings again?

Why does Barbara ring Rod? *She wants to invite him to* . . . .

Does Rod want to go? Why not? *No, because* . . . .

What excuse does Rod make first? *He says he's got* . . . .

What does Barbara suggest he does? *She suggests he* . . . .

What is Rod's next excuse? *He says he ought to* . . . .

What does Barbara now suggest? *She suggests that she and her friends* . . . .

What is Rod's final excuse? *He says he'd like to* . . . .

What do you think Barbara thinks? *She thinks Rod* . . . .

Do you think Rod wants to see Barbara again?

Invite people to do things
Refuse invitations politely and make excuses

The Invitations

Would you like to . . .

go out for a meal?
go to a disco?
go out for a walk?
go out for a drink?
go to the club?
go to the cinema?

come to a party?
come and play cards?
come round for a chat?
come round for a meal?
come to supper?
come and meet my friends?

Other things
. . . .
. . . .

. . . .
. . . .

The Excuses

Thanks very much. I'd love to but I'm afraid . . .

1. I've got a bad cold.
      a bad headache.
      a bad cough.
      a sore throat.
      . . . .
      . . . .

2. I've got to do some work.
      do my homework.
      go to a meeting.
      wait for an important
         phone call.
      . . . .
      . . . .

3. I ought to do my washing.
      get my things ready for
         tomorrow.
      write some letters.
      . . . .
      . . . .

4. I'd like to go to bed early.
      write some letters.
      make some phone calls.
      wash my hair.
      . . . .
      . . . .

1. **Work in pairs. Your partner invites you to do something; you make an excuse, choosing from** 1. *the list of illnesses.* **Like this:**

   Would you like to come to a party?
   That's very kind of you but I'm afraid I've got a bad cold.
   Oh, I *am* sorry. Some other time then?
   Yes, fine. But thanks for the invitation.

2. **Work in pairs. This time make excuses from** *groups* 2, 3 and 4. **Like this:**

   Would you like to go out for a meal?
   That's very kind of you, but I'm afraid I've got to do some work.
                              I ought to do my washing.
                              I'd like to go to bed early.

Oral Exercises

1.* **Ask people to ring you back and give a reason. Different people telephone you. You are busy. Look at page 55 to help you with your answers.**

Hello! It's Barbara here. Are you busy?
Well, actually, I'm (having supper) now. Could you ring me back later, Barbara?

Hi! This is Rod. Am I ringing at a bad time?
Well, actually, I'm (studying) now. Could you ring me back later, Rod?

Hello! It's Barbara here. Are you busy?

Hi! This is Rod. Am I ringing at a bad time?

Hello. This is Jack, Jack Cooper. Is this a good time to talk to you?

Hello. It's Joan here. Are you busy?

Good afternoon. This is Beautiful Homes Limited. Have you got a moment to spare?

2. **Confirm excuses**
You are working in an office. You explain to your boss why you and others want to leave work early.

What's your excuse this time? A headache?
Yes. I have got a very bad headache.

What's the matter with Helen? A cold, I suppose.
Yes, she has got a very bad cold.

What's your excuse this time? A headache?

What's the matter with Helen? A cold, I suppose.

Why isn't Richard here? A pain in his shoulder again?

Now Carol tells me she's got a headache. A headache!

Why does Jan want to go home? Don't tell me she's got a pain in her back again.

What's the matter with you? Is it your cough again?

3.* **Invite people to do things**
Try to persuade some friends to go out with you. Use the list of invitations on page 58.

Oh, dear. I've got to write some letters.
Really? Wouldn't you like to (go out for a meal) instead?

No, I ought to wash my hair.
Really? Wouldn't you like (to go out for a drink) instead?

Oh, dear. I've got to write some letters.
No, I ought to wash my hair.

I've got to get ready for tomorrow.
I'm going to write some letters.
I think I ought to study.
Oh, dear. I've got to do the washing.

4. **Repeat excuses**
A friend tries to persuade you to go out. You don't want to.

Oh, come on! One late night is all right. Let's go out.
I'd love to, but I really would like to go to bed early tonight.

We'll have a really great time. You can wash your hair tomorrow night.
I'd love to, but I really would like to wash my hair tonight.

Oh, come on! One late night is all right. Let's go out.

We'll have a really great time. You can wash your hair tomorrow night.

You can write some letters tomorrow. Why don't you come to the disco with us?

Come to the cinema with us—you can watch TV any time.

Oh, do let's go out. You can do the washing on Sunday.

You need to go out more. You can work tomorrow.

5.* **Make excuses**
Look at the list of excuses on page 58. Make your own excuses to a friend.

Couldn't I come round for a chat?
Sorry, but (I ought to do my washing).

But what about later?
Sorry, but (I'd like to go to bed early).

Couldn't I come round for a chat?

But what about later?

Shall we do something exciting this evening?

But what about having a meal together? I know —you could come round here.

All right. But couldn't I come round just for a few minutes—just for a chat—you know?

What about tomorrow evening then?

EXTENSION

1. Children's Hour

Imagine you are reading to a small child. This picture from a child's story book shows the Potter family: Mr and Mrs Potter, Sammy and Lucy, their dog, Spot, and their cat, Felix. Point to the people in the picture and describe them to the child in detail. Like this:

There's Mr Potter. He's in the kitchen. He's washing up.
Can you see a/the . . .?

bird
cat
dog

to chase
to ride

2. **Roleplay**
It is Sunday afternoon. You have nothing to do and are bored. Telephone a friend. Work in pairs.

YOU	YOUR PARTNER
	Answer the phone and say your name.
Say who you are.	Greet your friend.
Ask if your friend is busy and if you are ringing at a bad time.	Say you are busy and explain what you are doing.
Invite your friend to do something in the evening.	Refuse the invitation with thanks and make an excuse.
Accept the excuse, but repeat the same invitation for tomorrow evening.	Refuse again. Make an excuse for tomorrow by saying that you have something to do.
Accept and respond to the excuse.	Respond and say goodbye.
Say goodbye and say that you will ring some time next week.	

3. Mr and Mrs Hart received letters of *refusal* of the invitation to their party. Here are the last lines of four of the letters of refusal. Each letter states why the various people cannot accept the invitation. Because the invitation is formal, their replies are also formal.

Each of the people who wrote these letters also telephoned Mrs Hart to explain personally why they couldn't come to the party. Match each telephone conversation (1, 2, 3 or 4) with the right last line of the letters by putting a number 1, 2, 3 or 4 against it.

4. Imagine you also received an invitation to the Harts. Work in pairs. Your partner is Mr or Mrs Hart. Telephone him/her, thank him/her for the invitation and make an excuse for not coming.

Mr and Mrs James Hart
will be
AT HOME
on Friday March 6th
from 6.30—9.00p.m.

RSVP   4 Purley Road,
Burton,
Surrey
Tel. 253 6774

...... *because of a previous engagement.*

...... *owing to pressure of work.*

...... *due to family commitments.*

...... *is unfortunately ill in hospital.*

CHECK

Now you can:

1. Ask and talk about present actions

What are you doing?
I'm having a shower.

2. Invite people to do things

Would you like to go for a meal?

3. Refuse invitations politely

Thanks. I'd love to but . . .
That's very kind of you, but . . .

4. Make excuses

I'm afraid I've got a bad cold.
I'm afraid I've got to stay in.
I'm afraid I ought to write some letters.
I'm afraid I'd like to go to bed early.

5. Respond to excuses

All right. Some other time.

Grammar

What's	he she		He's She's I'm They're We're	having lunch. watching television. having a shower.
		doing?		
What are	you they			

Would you like to	go for a meal? go to the club? come to a party?

I've got to I ought to I'd like to	write some letters. go to bed early. relax at home.

Words and phrases

hair	ring back	definitely
baby	paint	just
shower	put somebody to bed	later on
card	entertain	at a bad time
chat	play (cards)	for once
cough	ride	to tell you the truth
sore throat	understand	some other time
meeting		See you around!
bicycle	busy	That sounds fun
bird	bad	
cat		

UNIT 9 Future plans

PEOPLE IN BUSINESS...

Pretty Feet– Pretty Future

This week's Bristol Business Personality:
Barbara Cooper, manageress of Pretty Feet.

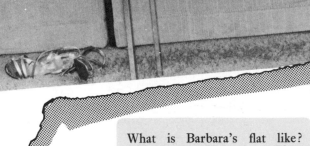

Working Girl
Ms. Cooper – 'call me Barbara' – was sitting on a new, very comfortable-looking sofa in her light and airy four-roomed flat in Bristol. She sipped her tea and looked relaxed. 'I'm just an ordinary working girl, really,' she said. I noticed her bare feet. 'I like selling shoes,' she explained. 'But I don't like wearing them much. I always take them off when I get home.'

Remarkable success
Still only in her mid-twenties, Barbara Cooper is already a remarkable success. From starting as a cashier in a local supermarket, she is now the manageress of a fashionable shoe-shop called 'Pretty Feet'.

All over Europe
'We sell shoes,' she said, to all sorts of people –young and old. But the younger market doesn't like wearing mass-produced British shoes, so I travel abroad a lot and buy lots of different designs from all over Europe.' Barbara travels widely. She makes about six trips abroad every year. Next week she is going to Italy to look at some of the new Italian designs.

Future Plans
And her plans for the future? Barbara explained: 'We're going to open branches in other cities. First London, then Manchester and Birmingham. After that, Leeds. Then we'll see how things go.'
We finished our tea and she showed me to the door. 'Come and see us in the shop one day,' she said, and then added, 'Remember, we sell shoes to all sorts of people.' Obviously things are going to turn out pretty well for Barbara Cooper.

Next week: Paul Gerrard–Pizza Prince

What is Barbara's flat like?
It's .... and .... There .... rooms.

Where was Barbara sitting?

Was Barbara wearing shoes?
......, her feet were ....

What was Barbara's first job?

What does she do now?

Why does Barbara buy lots of different designs from abroad?

How often does Barbara travel abroad? *......... times a year.*

Do you think the reporter was young?

Do you think Barbara's last remark was rude or amusing?

What time of day do you think it was?

* * *

What are Barbara's plans for next week? *She's going to ....*

What are her plans for the future?

What does the reporter think of Barbara's future? *She thinks things ....*

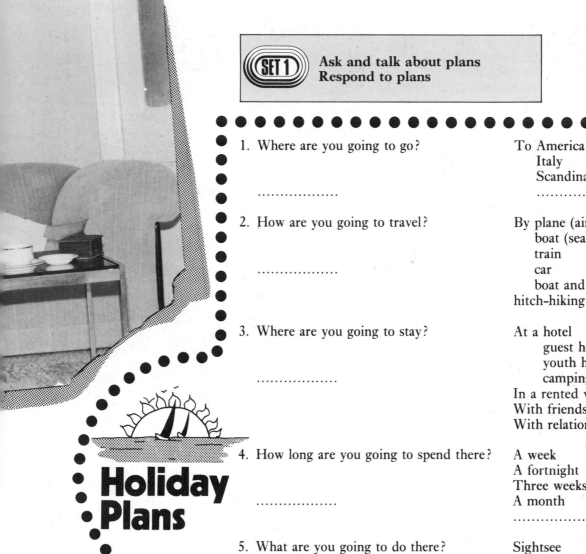

SET 1 Ask and talk about plans
Respond to plans

1. Where are you going to go?   To America
                                                Italy
                                                Scandinavia
....?

2. How are you going to travel?   By plane (air)
                                                   boat (sea)
                                                   train
....   car
                                                   boat and train
                               hitch-hiking

3. Where are you going to stay?   At a hotel
                                                     guest house
                                                     youth hostel
....   camping site
                                           In a rented villa
                                           With friends
                                           With relations

4. How long are you going to spend there?   A week
                                                     A fortnight
                                                     Three weeks
....   A month
                                             ....?

5. What are you going to do there?   Sightsee
                                                     Swim and lie on the beach
                                                 Visit friends
                                                   Go walking and climbing
....   Travel round the country
                                                     ....?

Holiday Plans

1. **Work in pairs.**
Imagine you are:

either a family with two children, aged 12 and 8
or   a young couple without children
or   a couple of students

You have £200 between you to spend on your next summer holiday.
Decide what you are going to do. Make notes.

Where are you going to go?	To Italy.	Really? How lovely!
How are you going to travel?	By car.	Oh, yes?
Where are you going to stay?	At a hotel.	That sounds fun.
How long are you going to spend there?	A week.	
What are you going to do there?	Sightsee.	

2. **Ask other pairs about their plans.**

A gang of thieves is going to rob a bank.
In the gang there are 3 men: Slick, Fingers, Velvet and 1 woman:
Marlene. Slick is the gang leader. He calls a meeting of the gang
the day before the robbery. He gives out the plans to each
member of the gang . . .

OPERATION MONEY BAGS

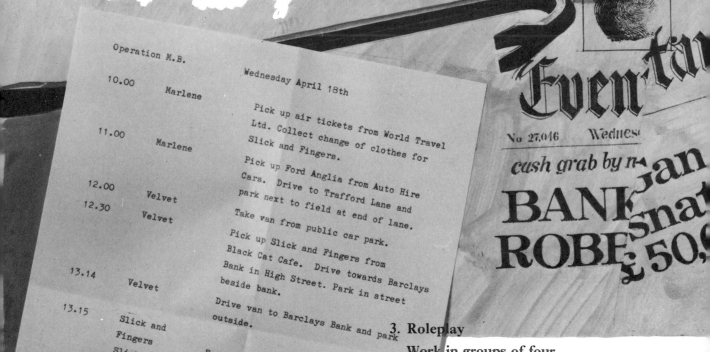

Operation M.B.

Wednesday April 18th

10.00	Marlene	Pick up air tickets from World Travel Ltd. Collect change of clothes for Slick and Fingers.
11.00	Marlene	Pick up Ford Anglia from Auto Hire Cars. Drive to Trafford Lane and park next to field at end of lane.
12.00	Velvet	Take van from public car park.
12.30	Velvet	Pick up Slick and Fingers from Black Cat Cafe. Drive towards Barclays Bank in High Street. Park in street beside bank.
13.14	Velvet	Drive van to Barclays Bank and park outside.
13.15	Slick and Fingers	
	Slick	Enter bank.
	Fingers	Guard doors.
13.20	Slick and Fingers	Take money.
	Velvet	
13.30	Slick and Fingers	Leave bank and get into van. Drive to Trafford Lane.
	Velvet	
13.35	Slick	Change clothes in back of van. Count money.
13.40	Marlene	Divide money.

Drive to Luton Airport to catch
15.30 plane to Miami...

3. Roleplay

Work in groups of four.
One of you is Slick. He calls the meeting. It is
Slick's job to check that every member of the
gang knows what he/she is going to do
during the robbery on the following day.
Start like this:

SLICK: Marlene—you start.
MARLENE: All right. At 10 o'clock I'm going to . . .

Give the rest of your plans.

4. **Now write an account of the bank robbery
plans in full.**
Link your sentences with *'and'*, *'then'*, *'after
that'*, *'an hour later'*.
Start like this:

At ten o'clock Marlene is going to pick up the
air tickets from . . .

Before Barbara left for Italy, she talked to her shop assistant, Gerry, about her plans, and reminded him to look after everything when she was away.

BARBARA: Gerry, I'm going to leave for the airport in half an hour. Can I have a word with you first?

GERRY: Yes, sure. How long are you going to spend in Italy, by the way?

BARBARA: Oh, just a week. I'm going to see some new designers this time, so it will be quite interesting. Now—you'll remember to check the till every evening, won't you?

GERRY: Yes, I will. Don't worry.

BARBARA: And you won't forget to lock all the doors when you leave?

GERRY: No, I won't. Relax, Barbara.

BARBARA: OK. Well, I must get ready. Oh, has Rod phoned this morning?

GERRY: No.

BARBARA: Oh. Oh, well. Look at the weather. It's going to rain again.

GERRY: What's the weather like in Italy at this time of year?

BARBARA: They say it's quite warm and sunny.

GERRY: Lucky you!

BARBARA: Gerry, don't forget I'm not going to have a holiday. I'm going there to work! Now, I think I ought to call a taxi . . .

When did Barbara talk to Gerry?

When is she going to leave for Italy?

What are her plans?

What does she remind Gerry to do?

Is the weather good in Bristol?

What's the weather like in Italy?

Is Barbara going to have a holiday in Italy?

Barbara talked to Gerry. Then she left for Italy.

=

Before Barbara left for Italy, she talked to Gerry.

(The time is 9.00.) I'm going to leave at 9.30.

=

I'm going to leave *in* half an hour.

A. Link these sentences with '*Before*'.

She checked the till. Then she locked the shop.

She talked to Gerry. Then she telephoned for a taxi.

She telephoned her parents. Then she left for Italy.

B. Make sentences using '*in*' like this:
Imagine the time is **9.00** and you are going to leave at:

9.10   I'm going to leave in ten minutes.
9.15
9.35
10.00
11.00

SET 2 **Remind people to do things**
Agree to do things

You'll remember to check the till, won't you?
You won't forget to lock all the doors, will you?
Yes, I will. Don't worry.
No, I won't. Don't worry.

1. **Work in pairs. A friend is going away on holiday. Remind him/her to do these things:**

> Lock front and back door
> Close all windows
> Turn off lights
> Turn off electric fires and fridge
> Cancel newspapers
> Tell police you are going away

Like this:

> You'll remember to lock the front and back door, won't you?
> Yes, I will. Don't worry.
> And you won't forget to........ , will you?
> No, I won't. Don't worry.

2. **Match the reminders with the pictures.**

1 Don't forget to lock your car doors!
2 Remember to cancel your newspapers when you go away on holiday!
3 Remember to look both ways when you cross the road!
4 Don't forget to fasten your seat belt!
5 Don't forget to check your passport before you go on holiday!

3. **How would you remind a friend who is:**

> going on a long car journey?
>   (check......take......)
> going to leave his house for 3 months?
>   (lock.........tell.........turn off.........)
> going for an interview for a job?
>   (be......wear......answer......ask......)
> going to take some children on a long train journey?   (take......wear......buy......)

Practise short conversations in pairs.

SET 3   Ask and talk about the weather

What's the weather like in Italy at this time of year?
They say it's sunny and warm.

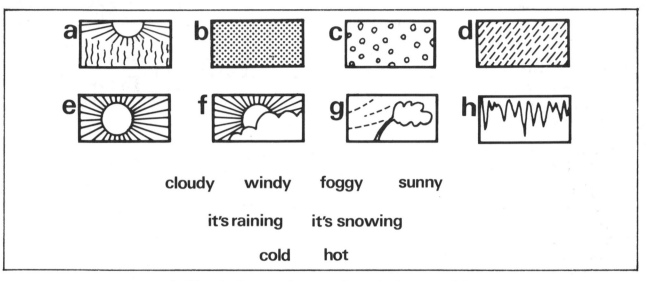

1. Match the weather words and phrases with the pictures.
2. Say what the weather is like in your area today.

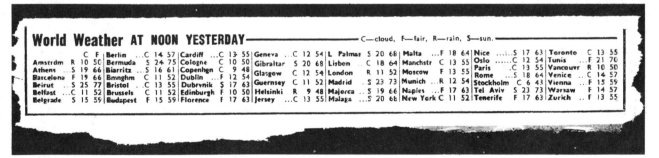

World Weather AT NOON YESTERDAY ———— C—cloud, F—fair, R—rain, S—sun. ——

	C F															
Amstrdm	R 10 50	Berlin ...C 14 57	Cardiff ...C 13 55	Geneva ...C 12 54	L Palmas S 20 68	Malta ...F 18 64	Nice ....)..S 17 63	Toronto C 13 55
Athens	...S 19 66	Bermuda S 24 75	Cologne C 10 50	Gibraltar S 20 68	Lisbon C 18 64	Manchstr C 13 55	Oslo ......C 12 54	Tunis ...F 21 70
Barcelona	F 19 66	Biarritz ...S 16 61	Copenhgn C 9 48	Glasgow C 12 54	London R 11 52	Moscow F 13 55	Paris ......C 13 55 / Rome ......S 18 64	Vancouvr R 10 50 / Venice C 14 57
Beirut	..S 25 77	Bmnghm C 11 52	Dublin ...F 12 54	Guernsey C 11 52	Madrid ...S 23 73	Munich ...R 12 54	Stockholm C 6 43	Vienna ...F 15 59
Belfast	...C 11 52	Bristol ..C 13 55	Dubrvnik S 17 63	Helsinki R 9 48	Majorca ...S 19 66	Naples ...F 17 63	Tel Aviv S 23 73	Warsaw F 14 57
Belgrade	S 15 59	Budapest F 15 59	Edinburgh F 10 50	Jersey ...C 13 55	Malaga ...S 20 68	New York C 11 52	Tenerife F 17 63	Zurich ...F 13 55

3. **Work in pairs. Look at the chart. Ask and answer like this:**

What's the weather like in Amsterdam?
Miserable! It's raining and cold.
What's the weather like in Malaga?
Lovely! It's sunny and quite hot.

Ask and answer about:

The capital of Greece   Two cities in Britain
Two cities in Italy   The capital of Yugoslavia
A city in Canada   A city in Spain
A capital city in   A city in Germany
   Scandinavia

4. **Work in pairs. Use the chart again. Ask and answer like this:**

What's the temperature in New York?
It's 11 degrees centigrade.
Oh, dear. That's rather cold!

or

What's the temperature in Malta?
It's 18 degrees centigrade.
That's nice and warm.

Oral Exercises

1. **Ask about people's travel plans**

   I'm going to Italy next week.
   Oh, are you? How long are you going to stay?

   Rod's going to Canada next July.
   Oh, is he? How long is he going to stay?

   I'm going to Italy next week.
   Rod's going to Canada next July.
   Jack's off to France soon.
   My daughter and her family are going to Spain for a holiday.
   Paul's making a trip to Germany next month.
   Barbara's going on business to Milan.

2. **Ask about people's accommodation plans**
   Look at the different kinds of accommodation in the chart on page 64.

   I'm going to spend the summer in Greece.
   Where are you going to stay? At a hotel?

   We're going to Bournemouth.
   Where are you going to stay? At a guest house?

   I'm going to spend the summer in Greece.
   We're going to Bournemouth.
   Lynne's going to the central part of France.
   The Ingrams are taking the family to Portugal by car.
   The Parkers have decided to have three weeks in southern Spain.
   Barbara's going to have a cheap holiday in Scotland.

3.* **Say what you are going to do or buy in different places**
   Look at the activities on page 64. They will help you with some of your replies.

   What are you going to buy when you go to Italy?
   I'm going to (buy some shoes).
   Oh, that's nice.

   What are you going to do when you go to the south of France?
   I'm going to (swim and lie on the beach).
   Oh, that sounds lovely.

   What are you going to buy when you go to Italy?
   What are you going to do when you go to the south of France?
   What are you going to do when you go to New York?
   What are you going to buy when you go to London?

   What are you going to do when you go to Scotland?

4. **Remind yourself to do things**
   You and your family are going away. You go through a list of reminders of things to do before you leave.
   Look at page 67.

   Remember the windows.
   Yes, I won't forget to shut them.

   Remember the door.
   Yes, I won't forget to lock it.

   Remember the windows.
   Remember the door.
   And the lights.
   Oh—and the newspapers.
   And the police.
   Oh, yes, and the fridge.

5. **Reassure people**

   Don't forget to shut the windows.
   No, don't worry. I won't.

   You'll remember to lock the door, won't you?
   Yes, don't worry. I will.

   Don't forget to shut the windows.
   You'll remember to lock the door, won't you?
   Please don't forget to post my letters.
   You will remember to phone me this evening, won't you?
   Before you go away, don't forget to get some travellers' cheques.
   Remember to buy me some stamps, won't you?

6. **Ask what the weather is like in different countries**

   I'm going to France in April.
   Oh yes, what's the weather like there in April?
   Oh, it's sometimes quite warm, I think.

   I'm going to Greece in February.
   Oh yes, what's the weather like there in February?
   Oh, it rains a lot.

   I'm going to France in April.
   I'm going to Greece in February.
   I'm going to Norway in the spring.
   I'm going to Egypt in October.
   I'm going to Scotland in March.
   I'm going to Argentina in July.

EXTENSION

LETTERS TO THE EDITOR

Who's going to pay?

Sir,
The government's plans for the country are certainly interesting. What are they going to do by the end of next year? They say they are going to build more day nurseries for working mothers. They say they are going to build more schools and increase grants for university students. Then they say they are going to reduce unemployment and improve the Health Service. Also they say they intend to reduce taxation.
Yes, it's a very interesting programme. But where is the government going to get the money for all this?
Well, I know the answer. The money is going to come out of the taxpayer's pocket. That's right! It's you and me who are going to pay.
Sir, may I suggest that, with the present state of the national economy, these plans are not only unrealistic, they're irresponsible!

M. C. Downing (Mrs)
Stockley, Manchester.

1. What is the Government going to do about day nurseries?
   What is it going to do about student grants?
   What is it going to do about unemployment?
   What about the Health Service?
   And what about taxation?
   What question does Mrs Downing ask?
   What is her answer?
   What does she think of the government's plans?

2. Listen to these people talking about their holiday plans to some friends. Fill in the details.

	Jane	Elizabeth
Country/Place		
Transport		
Length of stay		
Accommodation		
Activities		

Now write two short paragraphs describing their plans.
Like this:

Jane is going to . . .

3. **Roleplay**

   Work in pairs. Your partner is going on holiday. He plans to spend 3 weeks in a small hotel in Rome. The average temperature in Rome is 28 degrees centigrade. Talk to your partner about his holiday.

YOU	YOUR FRIEND
Ask where he is going	
	Say where
Respond and ask when he is going	
	Say when
Ask how long he is going to stay	
	Say how long
Respond and ask where he is going to stay	
	Say where
Respond and ask what the weather is like in Rome at the moment	
	Say what it's like
Remind him to send you a postcard	
	Agree to do this
Say you must go and say you hope your friend has a nice holiday	
	Say thank you and goodbye

4. The Ingrams plan to spend a day by the seaside at Weston-Super-Mare. Before they leave, they listen to the weather forecast for the day.

   Listen to the forecast and make notes about the weather. Then decide what activities would be best for the morning/at lunchtime/the afternoon. e.g. sunbathing? swimming? looking at the shops? having a picnic lunch? going to the cinema? going for a walk?

   What clothes should they take? Swimming things? Raincoats? Umbrellas?

CHECK

Now you can:

1. Ask and talk about plans
Where are you going to?
How long are you going to stay?
I'm going to go by car.

2. Respond to plans
Really! How lovely!
That sounds fun!

3. Remind people to do things
You'll remember to lock the door, won't you?
You won't forget to close the window, will you?

4. Agree to do things
Yes, I will. Don't worry.
No, I won't. Don't worry.

5. Ask and talk about the weather
What's the weather like (in Italy)?
Lovely. It's warm and sunny.
It's raining here and cold.
It's 15 degrees centigrade.

6. Link sentences with *before*
Before she left, she talked to Gerry.

Grammar

Where What How When How long	are / is	you they / he she	going to	go? do? travel? leave? spend there?

I'm He's She's We're They're	going to	go to Spain. lie on a beach. hitch-hike. leave in half an hour. spend a fortnight there.

You'll remember You won't forget	to close the windows,	won't you? will you?	Yes, I will. No, I won't.

Before she	left, phoned, locked up,	she	talked to Gerry. went to the bank. checked the till.

I'm leaving in	ten minutes. a quarter of an hour. three quarters of an hour. an hour.

Words and phrases

design	lane	sit	guard
future	sun	sell	count
cashier	designer	explain	divide
branch	umbrella	take off	forget
boat	capital	hitch-hike	check
guest house	degree	turn out	remember
villa	bare	fasten	tell
fortnight	fashionable	rain	cancel
centigrade	cloudy	snow	shut
field	windy	climb	still
	foggy	collect	already
		pick up	obviously

UNIT 10

GETTING UP TO DATE

A special feature for the Even Post
by Mike Sanders

Last week I found an old copy of Bristol Evening Post. In it were photographs of some of the p winners in the fifth form at Cli Park Comprehensive. I looked at t smiling faces and thought, 'I wo what they are doing now?'
Look below and you will see wh found out.

Name:	Barbara Cooper	Martha Hunt	John Murphy	Terry Fisher
Living in:	Bristol	Manchester	Aberdeen	Birmingham
Job:	Manageress of shoe shop in Bristol	Doctor at Manchester General Hospital	Engineer for an American Oil Company	Carpenter for a small building fir
Other news:	Barbara is studying shoe design at Bristol Technical College.	Martha is hoping to become an Ear, Nose and Throat specialist.	At the moment, John is working on an oil rig in the North Sea.	Terry is looking for a job in the car industry.

SET 1 Ask and talk about your present life

Name:	James Black	Clive Parker
Living in:	London	Madrid
Job:	Librarian at the North East London Polytechnic	English Language teacher in a large school in Madrid
Other news:	James is studying for a sociology degree.	Clive and his wife are expecting their first child.

1. Work in pairs. Ask and answer about the people in the article, like this:

Where is .... living now?
He's/She's living in ....
What is he/she doing now?
He's/She's ....
What other news is there about him/her?
He's/She's ....

2. Roleplay
Work in pairs. Act out two meetings:
   between Barbara and John
   between Martha and Clive.

Find out each other's news. Like this:

JOHN: Where are you living now, Barbara?
BARBARA: In Bristol. I'm the manageress of a shoe shop there.
JOHN: Oh, are you? Do you like the job?
BARBARA: Oh, yes. And I'm also studying shoe design at Bristol Technical College.
JOHN: That sounds interesting.
BARBARA: And what about you, John? Where are you living now?
JOHN: ....

3. Work in pairs. Ask each other about your own present lives.

4. Write a paragraph like this for Martha, John, Terry, James and Clive.

from the Clifton Park Comprehensive Old Students' Magazine:

Barbara Cooper is now living in Bristol where she is the manageress of shoe shop. In her spare time she is studying shoe design at Bristol Technic College.

73

Barbara Cooper is in Milan on a business trip. She is sitting in a small cafe outside the central station waiting to catch a train to Florence. Suddenly she sees an old school friend, Martha Hunt, walking past the cafe.

BARBARA: Martha!

MARTHA: Barbara!

BARBARA: What are you doing here? You live in Manchester, don't you?

MARTHA: Yes, that's right. I do. But I'm having a week's holiday here.

BARBARA: What? Here in Milan?

MARTHA: Yes, I'm visiting a friend. You know him actually— Roger.

BARBARA: Yes. I remember Roger.

MARTHA: Well, he's working here as a freelance journalist.

BARBARA: Is he? That must be fun.

MARTHA: Well, he says he's enjoying it. What about you? What are you doing here? Having a holiday as well?

BARBARA: No, not me. I'm working. I'm looking for some new shoe designs for the shop.

MARTHA: Oh, yes. I read about you in the Old Cliftonians' magazine. You're the manageress of a shoe shop now, aren't you?

BARBARA: Yes, that's right. It's doing quite well, in fact.

MARTHA: Which hotel are you staying at, by the way?

BARBARA: Well, I'm not staying in Milan any more. I'm catching the train to Florence in half an hour. In fact, I must go soon.

MARTHA: Oh, that's a pity. Anyway, I must go too. I must try and come and see you in Bristol one day.

BARBARA: Yes, do. And give my regards to Roger.

MARTHA: Yes, I will. Well—look after yourself and don't work too hard.

BARBARA: No, I won't. Have a nice holiday, by the way!

MARTHA: Thanks. Bye, Barbara!

Why is Barbara in Milan?

Where is she sitting when she meets Martha?

Why is she sitting there?

Who is Martha?

Who is Roger?

Does Barbara know him?

How does Martha know that Barbara is the manageress of a shoe shop?

When is Barbara leaving for Florence?

How is she going to travel?

* * *

Why is Martha in Italy?

Does Roger like his job as a freelance journalist?

What is Barbara doing in Milan?

Does Barbara say her shoe shop is successful? *Yes, she says it's ....* .

How many ways of saying goodbye can you find?

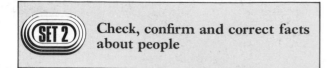

SET 2 Check, confirm and correct facts about people

Your name's Barbara Cooper, isn't it?	Yes, that's right.
You live in Bristol, don't you?	That's right. I do.
And you're the manageress of a shoe shop, aren't you?	Yes, I am. That's right.
You're studying for a degree in sociology, aren't you?	No. I'm studying shoe design.

1. **Roleplay**

   Work in pairs. You are Mike Sanders, the newspaper reporter. You interview the Old Cliftonians (page 73). Your partner is one of the Old Cliftonians.
   Check certain facts about his/her present life, using the information in the chart. Your partner confirms or corrects the facts. Start with Martha Hunt, like this:

   Your name is Martha Hunt, isn't it?
   Yes, ...
   And you live in Bristol, don't you?
   No, I ....
   Oh, yes. Sorry. But you're a doctor, aren't you?
   Yes, I ....

   Ask and answer in the same way about each person.

2. **Make notes about your partner. Write down five facts about him/her that you know or believe are true, e.g. his/her name, class, nationality, where he/she lives, his job, etc. Then work in pairs. Check your facts with your partner. Like this:**

   Your name is ...., isn't it?
   You're in class ...., aren't you?
   You're ...., aren't you?
   You live in ...., don't you?
   You're a ...., aren't you?
   ....

Glasgow is a city in Scotland, isn't it?	That's right.
Birmingham is by the sea, isn't it?	No, it isn't, actually.
English people drink a lot of instant coffee, don't they?	That's right.
TV programmes in England run all night, don't they?	No, they don't, actually.
It rains a lot in winter in Britain, doesn't it?	That's right.
Scotland produces a lot of coal, doesn't it?	No, it doesn't, actually.

3. **Confirm or correct these statements in the same way.**

   English policemen always carry guns, don't they?
   Scotland is famous for its whisky, isn't it?
   The river Thames flows through Bristol, doesn't it?
   In Britain they drive on the left hand side of the road, don't they?
   The capital of Scotland is Glasgow, isn't it?
   Ireland produces a lot of potatoes and butter, doesn't it?

4. **Make a list of 10 statements about countries —some true, some false. Ask your partner to confirm or correct them.**

A	B
I really must go now. Look, I must go now. Heavens! Look at the time— I must rush, I'm afraid.	Yes, I must go, too. Yes, I'm in a bit of a hurry, too.
Give my regards to Joe. Give my love to your parents. Look after yourself! Have a nice time! Enjoy yourself! Be good! Come and see us some time.	Yes, I will. Thanks. I will.
Don't work too hard. Don't forget to write. Don't drive too fast. Don't forget to phone me. Don't do anything I wouldn't do!	No, I won't. No. Don't worry. I won't.
Have a nice weekend. Have a lovely Christmas! Happy New Year!	Thanks. And the same to you!
Bye! See you! Goodbye! See you soon, I hope. Bye! See you on Monday! Goodbye! It was nice to meet you.	Yes, I hope so. Bye! Yes. See you soon! Yes. Bye! Yes. I hope we meet again some time. Goodbye!

1. **Work in pairs. Practise making and responding to parting remarks, using the tables. You read out a parting remark from column A; then your partner chooses a suitable response from column B. Like this:**

   I really must go now.
   Yes, I'm in a bit of a hurry, too.

Oral Exercises

1. **Answer questions about people's lives**
Look at page 73.

Do you know where Barbara's living now?
Yes, in Bristol.

Do you know what Martha's doing now?
Yes, she's a doctor in Manchester General Hospital.

Do you know where Barbara's living now?
Do you know what Martha's doing now?
Do you know where John Murphy's living now?
Do you know what Terry's doing now?
Do you know where James is living now?
Do you know what Clive Parker's doing now?

2. **Correct information about people's lives**
Look at page 73 again.

Barbara's living in Manchester, isn't she?
No, no, not Manchester. Bristol.

John's working in London, isn't he?
No, no, not London. Aberdeen.

Barbara's living in Manchester, isn't she?
John's working in London, isn't he?
Terry's working in Liverpool, isn't he?
Martha's living in Bristol, isn't she?
James is working in Scotland, isn't he?
Clive's living in Mexico, isn't he?

3. **Ask for precise information about people's lives**

Terry Fisher has got a job with a building firm.
Really! What exactly is he doing?
He's a carpenter, I think.

The Parkers are living in Spain.
Really! Where exactly are they living?
In Madrid, as far as I know.

Terry Fisher's got a job with a building firm.
The Parkers are living in Spain.
Paul's studying at the Polytechnic.
John's working for an oil company.
Terry and his wife are living in the Midlands.
Martha's working in a hospital.

4. **Express surprise about people's lives**
I'm working on an oil rig.
Oh, are you?

And my sister's living in America now.
Oh, is she?

Yes, and she likes it. But it's a long way from my parents. You see, they're living in France at the moment.
Oh, are they?

I'm working on an oil rig.
And my sister's living in America now.
Yes, and she likes it. But it's a long way from my parents. You see, they're living in France at the moment.
Yes, and you remember James. He's studying for a degree at present.
You know Clive? Well, he's working in Madrid now.
Yes, he and his wife are expecting their first child.

5. **Confirm and correct facts about people and places**

Barbara works in a shoe shop, doesn't she?
That's right, she does.

The shop's in the centre of Bristol, isn't it?
That's right, it is.

Rod works in a car factory, doesn't he?
No, he doesn't, actually. He works at Weston Aeronautics.

Barbara works in a shoe shop, doesn't she?
The shop's in the centre of Bristol, isn't it?
Rod works in a car factory, doesn't he?
But he works with Jack Cooper, doesn't he?
And Barbara is Jack Cooper's daughter, isn't she?
Barbara's living at home with her parents, isn't she?

6.* **Say goodbye in different ways**
Look at the different ways of saying goodbye on page 76.
Say goodbye to these people in the way you think best.

ROD: See you on Monday! Bye!
(Yes. Bye!)

PEGGY: Goodbye, and have a lovely weekend!
(Thanks and the same to you.)

See you on Monday! Bye!
Goodbye, and have a lovely weekend!
Cheerio! And enjoy yourself tonight!
I really must go now. Cheerio!
Bye! And don't forget to send me a postcard!
Have a good trip and look after yourself!

EXTENSION

1. **Peggy Cooper wrote a letter to her sister, Madge, who lives in Scotland. Peggy doesn't see her very often, so she wrote a long letter with all the family news.**

8 Belmont Crescent
Bristol 9
April 11th

Dear Madge,

Thank you so much for your long letter. It was lovely to hear all your news and get up to date. I am glad to hear that your backache is getting better and that the children are doing so well at school.

Now let me tell you all our news. Jack is still production manager at Weston. He's working very hard on a new order from Iran and there are lots of meetings all the time. He's very tired when he comes home at night. They're also having problems at the moment with pay demands. Jack says he's tired of it all. In fact, he's thinking of going to Toulouse to work for the new Weston branch there. We're still discussing whether to go or not. I don't really want to move away from all my friends here, but if Jack isn't happy, we've got to think seriously about it.

Barbara isn't living with us at home any more. She's got a flat of her own. Her shoe shop is doing very well and she's travelling abroad a lot, so we don't see much of her. She's in Italy at the moment, but I don't know exactly what she's doing there. She's got a new boyfriend who works at Weston with Jack. He's very nice — Canadian — but I don't think it's very serious. Barbara was never keen on settling down, you know.

As for me, I'm now working only part-time at the office. I'm also taking French lessons. I'm starting from the beginning again! It's great fun and I'm meeting lots of different sorts of people.

Well, I'm going to try and catch the last post, so I'll stop now.
All the best from us both,
Love to you and the family,

Peggy

What news do you learn about the following people:

Madge?
Her children?
Jack?
Barbara?
Peggy?

2. **Write a letter to an old friend of your family. Give news about yourself and other members of the family.**
   Don't forget to ask for news about your friend and his/her family.

3. **Listen to some international scientists talking about their present research activities. Fill in the chart with the correct information.**

	Dr Pierre Chabrol	Dr Brian Powers	Dr Carmen Hernandez
Subject:			
Place:			
University:			

Now write a short paragraph about one of the scientists for a scientific journal. Start like this:

Dr Chabrol is at present investigating ………

4. **Roleplay**

Work in pairs. You are in the street and you see a friend you haven't met for some time.

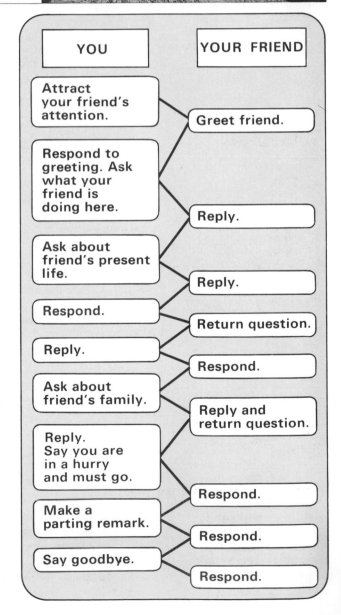

YOU	YOUR FRIEND
Attract your friend's attention.	
	Greet friend.
Respond to greeting. Ask what your friend is doing here.	
	Reply.
Ask about friend's present life.	
	Reply.
Respond.	
	Return question.
Reply.	
	Respond.
Ask about friend's family.	
	Reply and return question.
Reply. Say you are in a hurry and must go.	
	Respond.
Make a parting remark.	
	Respond.
Say goodbye.	
	Respond.

CHECK

Now you can:

1. Ask about people's present lives

Where are you living now?
What are you doing now?

2. Talk about your present life

I'm living in Bristol now.
I'm working at the hospital.

3. Check facts

Your name's Clive, isn't it?
You're English, aren't you?
You work in Madrid, don't you?

4. Confirm facts

Yes, that's right. It is.
Yes, that's right. I am.
Yes, that's right. I do.

5. Correct facts

No, it isn't, actually.
No, I'm not, actually.
No, I don't actually.

6. Make and respond to parting remarks

I really must go now.
Look after yourself.
Bye! See you!
Yes, I must go too.
Yes, I will.
Yes, I hope so. Bye!

Grammar

Are	you they	living in Bristol?	I'm not We aren't They aren't	living in Bristol.
Is	he she		He isn't She isn't	

You're They're	English,	aren't	you? they?	Yes, that's right.	I am. They are.
He's She's It's		isn't	he? she? it?		He is. She is. It is.

You They He She	work	in Bristol,	don't	you? they?	I do. They do.
	works		doesn't	he? she?	He does. She does.

Words and phrases

face	carpenter	problem	instant	It was nice	build	pay for
ear	firm	pay demand	seriously	meeting	expect (a child)	settle down
nose	librarian	pronunciation	any more	you	get up to date	rush
throat	degree (education)	regards	Be good!	smile	discuss	hear
specialist	sociology	at present	The same	hope	catch (post/train)	
oil rig	meeting	fast	to you!	become	do well	

1. Read and complete these conversations.

1. A: I'm going to Greece for a week in May.
   B: ....
   A: They say it's quite warm, but not really warm enough to swim.

2. A: ....
   B: This afternoon? I'm going to stay at home and work in the garden.

3. A: ....
   B: Really? I thought you liked the job. What are you going to do instead?

4. A: ....
   B: No, we finished all the eggs yesterday.

5. A: What have we got in the fridge?
   B: .... That's all.
   C: Oh, well, let's have a cheese omelette then.

6. A: ....
   B: No, don't worry. I won't. I always lock it when I leave.

7. A: Would you like to go out for a walk with us?
   B: ....
   A: Oh, have you? I *am* sorry. Why don't you take an aspirin and lie down?

8. A: Do you feel like going out this evening?
   B: ....
   A: But your hair looks all right to me.

9. A: Am I ringing at a bad time?
   B: ....
   A: Are you sure? I can phone back when the programme is over if you like.

10. A: ....
    B: My brother? Oh, he's working in a hotel in Singapore.
    A: ....
    B: For about six months, I think.

11. A: New York is the capital of America, isn't it?
    B: ....

12. A: ....
    B: Yes, I hope we meet again some time.

2. A special dinner

You are going to cook a special dinner this evening. In your fridge and food cupboard at home there is:

chicken stock	rice
onions	salt
butter	pepper
flour	oranges
	cheese

And these are the ingredients for Chicken Blanquette:

> 1 chicken
> 1 onion
> 250gm. mushrooms
> ½ litre chicken stock
> 100gm. butter
> 100gm. flour
> 2-3 tablespoons cream
> a few drops of lemon juice
> salt and pepper

This is your dinner menu:

> Tomato juice
> ...
> Chicken Blanquette
> Rice
> Tomato Salad   White wine
> ...
> Cheese

Work in pairs. One of you makes a list of all the food you will need to prepare the dinner. The other has the list of food that you have already got in the house.

Ask and answer like this:

Have we got any tomato juice?
No, we haven't.
Oh, well, let's get some tomato juice then.

Make a list of all the things you need to buy. Then read your list out like this:

We need some ...., a ...., some .... and some ....

3. Roleplay
   Work in pairs. A friend comes to see you at
   home. It is quite late in the evening. He/She
   has just been to an English class and is very
   hungry.

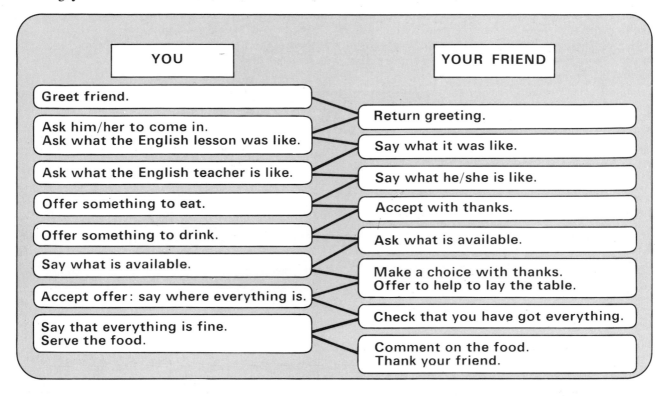

YOU	YOUR FRIEND
Greet friend.	Return greeting.
Ask him/her to come in. Ask what the English lesson was like.	Say what it was like.
Ask what the English teacher is like.	Say what he/she is like.
Offer something to eat.	Accept with thanks.
Offer something to drink.	Ask what is available.
Say what is available.	Make a choice with thanks. Offer to help to lay the table.
Accept offer: say where everything is.	Check that you have got everything.
Say that everything is fine. Serve the food.	Comment on the food. Thank your friend.

WARNINGS! How to stop accidents in the home!

Remember to Always Don't forget to	put away keep them away from	sharp knives (after using them). scissors (after using them). electrical equipment when it's on. plugs and sockets. boiling water.
Never	let them touch let them go near	fires when they're on. the iron when it's on. the cooker when it's on.

4. Most accidents with small children happen in the home.
   What reminders and warnings can you give to parents of small children?
   Make a list of warnings from the chart. Like this:

   Remember to put away sharp knives after using them.
   Don't leave electrical equipment when it's on.
   Never let them go near fires when they're on.

   Make as many sentences as you can.

5. Roleplay
Work in pairs. One of you is Rod. The other is Lynne.

One Friday afternoon after work, Rod decides that he wants to spend a day in the country—driving around, walking, seeing the local sights, having lunch in a country pub and so on.

Barbara is away in Italy, so he telephones Lynne to see if she would like to come with him—either on Saturday or Sunday.

In fact, Lynne has already planned to do other things at the weekend, so she cannot accept. This is the page from her diary for Saturday and Sunday.

Act the telephone conversation between Lynne and Rod. Rod must try very hard to persuade Lynne to come. Lynne must make her excuses for not coming.

saturday

11 a.m.	Hair Appointment
2.30	Visit Granny in hospital – do washing
8.00	Party at Mary's (get birthday present)

sunday

Lunch with Mum and Dad
cinema with Julie at 4pm.
evening – GO TO BED EARLY !!!

6. Complete the conversation

Rod is talking to Paul, his flat-mate, one Friday evening. Paul is studying. They talk a little about Paul's studies and what he is going to do after he has finished at the Polytechnic. Paul asks Rod about his plans—and Barbara's—for the future.

ROD: ....? (*What/read*)

PAUL: Oh, it's a book about naval engineering.

ROD: .... on a Friday evening? (*Why/read*)

PAUL: Because I've got to write an essay this weekend.

ROD: .... when you're qualified? (*What/do*)

PAUL: I don't know. I'd like to get a job abroad, I think. .... when your year at Weston is over? (*What/do*)

ROD: I'm going to spend a few weeks touring Britain, then I'm going back to Canada, I suppose.

PAUL: .... (*What/Barbara/do*)

ROD: I think she's going to open a branch of 'Pretty Feet' in London.

PAUL: .... in Italy? (*What/she/do*)

ROD: She's seeing some designers there. She's coming back tomorrow. By the way, ... on Saturday evening? (*What/you and Sue/do*)

PAUL: I don't know yet. Why?

ROD: Well, I thought we could cook another of our famous suppers and invite Barbara and Sue.

PAUL: Oh, no! Not Potato Salad again! Sorry, Rod, but I really have to read this book.

7. Paul Blake, who is also an Old Cliftonian, received this letter from his old headmaster.

CLIFTON COMPREHENSIVE SCHOOL
Clifton, Bristol

Dear Old Cliftonian,
As you may know, we are having a reunion for Old Cliftonians on May 26th
from 2 p.m. – 6 p.m. We would be delighted if as many old pupils as possible
could attend. Could you please let me know if you can or cannot attend as
soon as possible?
I would also be grateful if you could send in a few lines saying what you are
doing at the present moment. All news of Old Cliftonians will be printed in
the annual school magazine, in June this year.

With many thanks in advance
Yours sincerely
John Fowler
John Fowler
Headmaster

Imagine you are Paul Blake.

i) Write a letter refusing the invitation to the reunion, giving an excuse. Start like this:

Dear Mr Fowler,
Thank you very much for your invitation to ……… on ………. I would love to come, but I'm afraid I ………

ii) Write another paragraph at the end of the letter, saying what you are doing now (your studies, where you are living, what you would like to do in the future).

LOOKING FOR A BIGGER MARKET

Report by Simon Lister

WESTON AERONAUTICS LIMITED, a company based in Bristol, is planning to enter the European market. At the moment, Weston are producing small electrical components. In fact, they are making all the cabin lighting equipment for the British Aircraft Corporation. As part of the future development of the company, the Weston board of directors are now setting up a second factory in Toulouse, France.

Peter Chester, managing director of Weston, is at present living in Toulouse for a six month period, where he is studying the needs of the French aircraft industry.
'I want to avoid problems later on, so I am making a very detailed investigation. The French authorities are being very helpful. Back in Bristol, we are now looking for skilled craftsmen and people on the production side to go with their families to work in Toulouse. I don't think we are going to have any problems finding staff. Most people enjoy a challenge.'

8. Use the article to make a list of the questions the reporter asked to get these answers from Peter Chester:

1. I'm the managing director at Weston.
2. In Bristol.
3. All the cabin lighting equipment for the British Aircraft Corporation, for example.
4. We're setting up a second factory in Toulouse. *(How is Weston planning to …?)*
5. I'm studying the needs of the French aircraft industry, mainly.
6. For about six months.
7. Oh, yes, very helpful indeed....
8. That's right, skilled craftsmen and production people.
9. No, I don't. Most people enjoy a challenge.

Now work in pairs. Use the questions and the answers and act out the interview between Simon Lister and Peter Chester.

9. Game: Categories

	B	S	T
Country:	Belgium		
City:	Bristol		
Name:	Barbara		
Singer or group:	Beatles		
Name of car:	Buick		
Food:	Bread		
Drink:	Beer		
Sport:	Badminton		

You have 5 minutes!
Find names or words beginning with S and T to fit each category.

At the arrival gate at London Airport.

ROD: Hello, Barbara! Welcome back! You look marvellous!

BARBARA: Rod! What a surprise! It's lovely to see you again.

ROD: Sorry I didn't telephone you before you left, but I didn't have time, in fact . . .

BARBARA: Oh, that's all right. Forget it!

ROD: Well, how was Italy?

BARBARA: Fun, but tiring. Milan was interesting. It's bigger than I expected. Noisier and dirtier, too.

ROD: And Florence? What did you think of Florence?

BARBARA: Well, I've never been there before. I thought it was beautiful. More beautiful than Paris, in fact. Have you ever been to Italy?

ROD: No, never. I'd really like to go to Rome. Well, the car's in the car park. Is this all your luggage?

BARBARA: Yes, but the suitcase is very heavy.

ROD: Barbara! What's in it? Stones?

BARBARA: No. Just twenty pairs of shoes! Oh, it *is* nice to see you again, Rod!

HOME AGAIN!

SET 1 — Give apologies and explanations
Accept apologies

Sorry I didn't telephone you, but I didn't have time.
Oh, that's all right. Forget it!

Apologise for:

a) not doing your homework—

b) missing the train—

c) not writing while you were away—

d) not meeting your friend at the station—

Explanations

you { forgot / didn't have time / lost your book

you { overslept / couldn't get a taxi
your { watch was slow / timetable was out of date

you { forgot / were very busy / lost the address

you { overslept / got the time of arrival wrong
your car didn't start

Where did Rod meet Barbara?
Where is Rod's car?
Why is Barbara's suitcase heavy?
Is Barbara pleased to see Rod?
* * *
Why didn't Rod telephone Barbara before she left?
What did he say when he apologised? *Sorry I ....
but ....* .
What did Barbara think of Italy? *She thought it was .... but ....* .
What did she think of Milan?
Has Rod ever been to Italy?
......, he .... He's never ....
Have you ever been to Italy?

Can you think of a country/town that is more beautiful/bigger/smaller/livelier than yours?

---

1. **Work in pairs. Make apologies, choosing different explanations, to your partner. Your partner accepts your apology. Like this:**
   Sorry I didn't do my homework, but I forgot.
   Oh, that's all right.

2. **Roleplay**
   Work in pairs.
   a) Apologise and explain to your teacher why you didn't come to classes last week.
   b) Apologise and explain to your mother why you didn't do the washing-up last night.
   c) Apologise and explain to a friend why you didn't write or telephone him/her while you were away in London.
   d) Apologise and explain to your boss why you arrived half an hour late for work this morning.

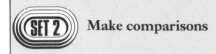

SET 2   **Make comparisons**

Milan is bigger than I expected. Noisier and dirtier, too.
I think Florence is more beautiful than Paris.

FACTS ABOUT PLACES, PEOPLE AND THINGS

size		height		length		temperature	
big	bigger	tall	taller	long	longer	hot	hotter
large	larger	high	higher	wide	wider	warm	warmer
small	smaller	short	shorter			mild	milder
						cool	cooler
						cold	colder

OPINIONS ABOUT PLACES, PEOPLE AND THINGS

dirty	dirtier	lively	livelier	bad	worse
clean	cleaner	dull	duller	fast	faster
noisy	noisier	cheap	cheaper	slow	slower
ugly	uglier	good	better		

beautiful	more beautiful
interesting	more interesting
depressing	more depressing
expensive	more expensive
exciting	more exciting

---

1. **Compare the features of countries like this:**
   China/large/Japan   China is larger than Japan.
   England/small/France
   London/big/Rome
   Skyscrapers in New York/tall/buildings in London
   The River Avon/short/the Thames
   The Mississippi/long/the Nile
   Mount Everest/high/Kebeknaise

   The South of France/hot/the North
   The Mediterranean/warm/the North Sea
   The air at night/cool/the sea at night
   Winters in Scandinavia/cold/the winters in Western Europe
   English winters/mild/Scottish winters
   The Aegean/warm/the Baltic

2. **Compare your country with any other country you know well.**
   Compare these features:

size	roads	geographical features
climate	people	(mountains, rivers,
cities and towns	food	lakes)
the standard of living		*anything else*

3. **Work in pairs. Read your comparisons to your partner. Your partner agrees, disagrees or responds like this:**
   Spain is larger than Portugal.
   Yes, that's true.
   And the people in Portugal are livelier than the people in Spain.
   Yes, I agree. *or* No, I don't agree. I think the people in Spain are livelier.
   But the food in Spain is more expensive than the food in Portugal.
   Really? That's interesting. I didn't know that.

 **SET 3** **Ask and talk about experiences and impressions**

Have you ever been to Italy?
Yes, I have. I went there last summer, actually.
Did you enjoy it?
I thought it was marvellous!

Have you ever eaten snails?
No, never. Have you?
Yes, once, when I went to a French restaurant.
What did you think of them?
Actually, I didn't like them very much.

1. **Work in pairs. Ask and talk about these things:**

TRAVEL

Have you ever been to...?
Did you enjoy it?

Examples
France
The Far East
Britain
Europe
................?

ACTIVITIES
AND SPORTS

Have you ever done any...?
Do/did you enjoy it?
How did you get on?

sailing
waterskiing
horseriding
fishing
hitch-hiking
camping
skate-boarding
carpentry
dressmaking
mountain climbing
................?

FOOD AND
DRINK

Have you ever { tried...?
eaten...?
drunk...? }
Did you like it?
What did you think of it?

Indian food
Chinese food
snails
Guinness
bourbon
raw fish
................?

2. **Work in pairs. Make a list of films you have both seen recently.**

YOU	YOUR PARTNER
Ask if your partner has seen............ (name of film).	
	Answer.
Ask for opinion of film.	
	Give opinion. Ask if partner has seen.......... (name of another film).
Answer.	
	Ask for opinion.
Give opinion.	
	Agree or disagree.

Mona Laird is a friend of Barbara's. She's a short story writer for a popular women's magazine. She often writes romantic serials. Here is a short chapter which she wrote for one story.

Clarissa

Continuing our romantic serial:

For new readers—Clarissa Hooper is on her way back to England after a visit to Italy . . . Read on.

CLARISSA looked out of the taxi window at the wet road. It was still raining. She was looking forward to getting home after a busy and tiring week in Italy.

The taxi began to slow down. Then the brown-eyed driver turned to Clarissa and said, 'Terminal, signora.' He smiled. The taxi stopped outside the terminal and Clarissa got out. While she was finding some money in her purse, the driver took out her luggage. 'The last of my lira,' thought Clarissa sadly.

The rain stopped. 'Here's your change,' said the driver in English. 'No, you keep it, please,' said Clarissa with a smile. Then she went inside the terminal building.

The British Airways check-in desk was near the entrance. After checking in her luggage, she went to buy some magazines. Then she went through passport control and into the Departure Lounge.

There was half an hour before her flight left. While she was waiting she bought some cigarettes and some duty-free brandy for her father. She thought suddenly of Simon. 'Perhaps I ought to buy something for Simon. But he never telephoned me before I left, so . . .'

'British Airways announce the departure of Flight BA 677 to London Heathrow. Will all passengers please proceed to Gate 11. Flight BA 677 to London Heathrow is now boarding.'

It was time to leave. After waiting in the queue with the other passengers, Clarissa got her seat number and walked onto the plane. Her seat was next to the window—and the emergency exit. With relief she sat down and fastened her safety belt. But she still felt nervous. She often travelled by plane, but she still hated every moment of it.

When the plane was taking off, she closed her eyes, but when the plane was in the air, she began to relax. She thought about Simon. She hadn't sent him a postcard, but he hadn't even telephoned her to say goodbye!

'I wonder if he's going to come and meet me at the airport. It's so much nicer to come home when there's someone to meet you and help with your luggage. All those pairs of shoes. They're heavier than I expected. Anyway, I don't really care if he's there or not.'

When the plane came to a standstill, Clarissa saw that outside the sun was shining.

Complete the details of Clarissa's departure from Milan airport with the words in the box.

1. Clarissa......... at the .... by taxi.
2. Then she went to the British Airways .... desk.
3. She .... her ....
4. Then she went to buy some magazines for the ....
5. After that she went through ....
6. In the .... lounge she bought some .... goods.
7. Soon she heard the announcement: 'Will all .... please proceed to .... 11.'
8. At the departure gate she collected her ....
9. On the .... she found that her seat was next to the window and the ....
10. She fastened her .... and waited nervously for the plane to ....

check-in   duty-free   checked in   emergency exit
journey   take off   luggage   arrived   passport control
seat number   seat belt   terminal   plane   departure
passengers   gate

SET 4 Narrate and link past events

Before/After

First she checked in her luggage.
Then she went to buy some magazines.
=
Before buying some magazines, she checked in her luggage.
=
After checking in her luggage, she went to buy some magazines.

1. **Link these pairs of sentences in two ways. First use** '*Before ......ing*'. **Then use** '*After ......ing*'.
   1. First she bought some magazines. Then she went through passport control.
   2. First she bought some duty-free brandy. Then she went to the departure lounge.
   3. First she collected her seat number. Then she boarded the plane.

While

She waited for her flight to be called.
At the same time she bought some duty-free brandy.
=
While she was waiting for her flight to be called, she bought some duty-free brandy.

2. **Link these pairs of sentences with** '*While ...... was ......ing*'.
   1. Clarissa looked for some money. The driver got out her luggage.
   2. She waited in the departure lounge. She had a cup of coffee.
   3. The plane took off. Clarissa closed her eyes.

When

The plane came to a standstill.
She saw that the sun was shining.
=
When the plane came to a standstill, she saw that the sun was shining.

3. **Link these pairs of sentences with** '*When*'.
   1. She found that her seat was near the Emergency Exit. She sat down with relief.
   2. The plane took off. She felt nervous.
   3. The plane was in the air. She began to relax.

4. **Write an account of Clarissa's arrival at London airport. Link these events with** *when, while, before, after* **and** *then*.

Clarissa's arrival

Clarissa:
    waited for most of the passengers to get off.
    unfastened her seat belt.
    picked up her hand luggage.
    left the plane.
    went through passport control.
    waited for her luggage.
    (at the same time) phoned her parents.
    found a luggage trolley.
    collected her luggage.
    went through Customs.
    saw Simon waiting at the arrival gate.

Oral Exercises

1. Apologise and give an explanation

You didn't have time to send your friend a post-card.

Sorry I didn't send you a postcard, but I didn't have time.

That's OK.

You forgot to telephone your friend.

Sorry I didn't telephone, but I forgot.

That's all right.

You didn't have time to send your friend a post-card.

You forgot to telephone your friend.

You overslept so you missed the bus. Apologise to your boss.

Your watch was slow and you were late for work. Apologise to your boss.

You were ill last week, so you didn't come to classes. Apologise to your teacher.

You didn't know the time of the train, so you didn't meet your sister at the station.

2. Make comparisons about the weather
You have been to different parts of the world. Talk about the weather.

What was the weather like in Cairo? Hot, I suppose?

Yes, it was much hotter than we expected.

So you went to the south of France for Christmas? Well, they say it's quite mild there.

Yes, it was much milder than we expected.

What was the weather like in Cairo? Hot, I suppose?

So you went to the south of France for Christmas? Well, they say it's quite mild there.

What was the winter like in the Soviet Union? Cold?

I hear you were in Ireland last month. I'm sure the weather was wet.

So you spent the winter in Mexico? Was the weather cool?

Was the weather warm in England when you were there?

3. Compare experiences
You have just come back from your holiday in Spain. You always go there every year. Look at the list of adjectives on page 87.

What was the weather like? Good?

Yes, much better than last year.

And what about the shops? Were they expensive?

Yes, much more expensive than last year.

What was the weather like? Good?

And what about the shops? Were they expensive?

And the sea? Was it nice and clean?

But were the beaches crowded?

Were the people at the hotel interesting?

And what about the food? Was it bad again?

4. Give a contrasting comparison
You have been on holiday with friends. Match the pairs of opposite adjectives to make your comparisons.

good	cheap	exciting	beautiful
interesting	dirty	dull	ugly
expensive	clean	bad	depressing

The food was better than I expected.

Well, I thought it was rather bad.

Did you? Well, the discos were exciting.

Well, I thought they were rather depressing.

The food was better than I expected.

The discos were exciting.

Mind you, the drinks were expensive.

And the beaches were a bit dirty.

Still, I thought the countryside was interesting.

At least the modern hotels were really beautiful.

5. Ask about people's experience
Ask about pictures 1–6.

1 *Have you ever done any horse riding?*
   Yes, I have. Once.
   How did you get on?
   Quite well, in fact.

2 *Have you ever done any sailing?*
   Yes, I do a lot of sailing.
   Oh, do you enjoy it?
   Yes, very much.

EXTENSION

1. **What comparisons would you make to a friend who can't decide between:**

1 a boating holiday
down the Rhine   AND   a hitch-hiking holiday
in the English Lake District?

(useful adjectives: beautiful, warm, cold, cheap, relaxing)

2 dinner in a
French restaurant   AND   dinner in an
Indian restaurant?

(expensive, tasty, simple, spicy, interesting, ordinary)

3 travelling by train
through Germany   AND   travelling by car
through Germany?

(cheap, fast, comfortable, relaxing)

4 a career
as a doctor   AND   a career
as a dentist?

(interesting, well-paid, rewarding)

5 a job as an
air steward   AND   a job as a
social worker?

(exciting, interesting, rewarding)

6 taking up squash   AND   taking up tennis?

(energetic, sociable, difficult, fun)

Make comparisons like this:

It's warmer in Germany than in the Lake District.
Indian food is tastier than French food. It's cheaper, too.

2. **John is British, but he has worked in Japan. Etsuko is Japanese from Osaka, but she is studying in Britain.**
Listen to them comparing life as they see it in the two countries. Make notes about the features of each country they mention and the comparisons they make.

	THE FEATURES	COMPARISONS
John:	The people in Japan are	....
	....	
Etsuko:	The summer in England is	....
	....	

Write paragraphs using your notes, like this:
John says that, in his experience, the ....
Etsuko says that, in her experience, the ....

3. **Work in pairs. First complete the following questions from your own experience:**

Have you ever been to a party when (people danced all night)?
Have you ever been in a car when ....?
Have you ever been in an embarrassing situation when ....?
Have you ever had the sort of dream when ....?
Now ask your partner if he/she has had a similar experience.

4. **Think of a journey you have made recently.**

First make notes of the things you did and the things that happened.

Then write about your journey, using the linking words *before*, *after*, *while* and *when*.

Read the account of your journey to your partner.

CHECK

Now you can:

1. Give apologies and explanations	Sorry I didn't telephone you, but ………
2. Accept apologies	That's all right! Forget it!
3. Make comparisons	Milan is bigger than I expected. Florence is more beautiful than Milan.
4. Agree, disagree and respond to statements	Yes, that's true. Yes, I agree. No, I don't agree. I think ……… Really? That's interesting. I didn't know that.
5. Ask and talk about experiences and impressions	Have you ever ………? Yes, I have./No, never. Have you? What did you think of it? Did you like it?
6. Narrate and link past events with *Before, After, While and When*	Before buying some magazines, she checked in her luggage. After checking in her luggage, she went to buy some magazines. While she was waiting for her flight, she bought some brandy. When the plane came to a standstill, she saw that the sun was shining.

Grammar

Scotland France	is	colder livelier more beautiful	than	England. Spain.

Have you ever	been to Spain? eaten Indian food? done any fishing?

Yes,	I have. once.
No,	never.

Before After	checking in her luggage	he she they	bought a magazine. boarded the plane.

While	he she was	waiting, looking,	the driver he she	collected her/his luggage. had a cup of coffee.

When	she he the plane	arrived, stopped,	she he the passengers	began to relax. got off.

Words and phrases

luggage	passport control	career	nervous	slow down
pair	customs	dentist	dirty	skateboard
dressmaking	trolley	social worker	simple	fish
carpentry	relief	cool	relaxing	oversleep
purse	air	mild	ordinary	sail
check-in desk	skyscraper	tall	rewarding	miss
departure lounge	snail	long	energetic	check in
seat belt	squash	wide	sociable	lose

UNIT 13
MANDY IS MISSING

At Clifton Police Station. The telephone rings . . .

POLICEMAN: Clifton Police Station. Can I help you?

MRS INGRAMS: Yes. It's about my daughter, Mandy. She went to school this morning and she hasn't arrived home yet, and it's eleven o'clock and . . .

POLICEMAN: Just a moment, Mrs . . .?

MRS INGRAMS: Mrs Ingrams. Joan Ingrams, 57 Bath Road.

POLICEMAN: Thank you. Now Mrs Ingrams, what exactly is the matter?

MRS INGRAMS: Well, Mandy—that's my little daughter—left home this morning at about a quarter to nine. Then her teacher telephoned me about a quarter of an hour ago and asked if Mandy was ill. I said, 'No. Why?' And then she said, 'Well, Mandy hasn't come to school yet.' So I said I didn't know where she was. Then I decided to ring you.

POLICEMAN: Quite right. Perhaps she went home to a friend? Have you asked your neighbours?

MRS INGRAMS: Yes, I have. I've rung all the neighbours and they haven't seen her, and their children are all at school and . . .

POLICEMAN: I see. Now, let's have a few details. How old is Mandy?

MRS INGRAMS: She's six.

POLICEMAN: And what does she look like?

MRS INGRAMS: She's got fair hair, long fair hair with a ribbon in it —a red ribbon—er—she's got blue eyes . . .

POLICEMAN: And what's she wearing?

MRS INGRAMS: She's wearing a grey coat and brown shoes, red tights—er—a green skirt and a red sweater. Yes, that's right.

POLICEMAN: We'll do our best to find her, Mrs Ingrams. I expect she's just playing truant. Now you keep calm and we'll telephone you as soon as we find her.

MRS INGRAMS: Thank you. Goodbye.

POLICEMAN: Goodbye, Mrs Ingrams. And try not to worry.

A. Use the dialogue to complete the police form.

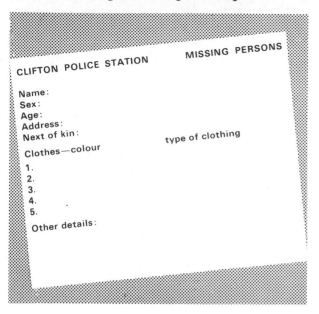

CLIFTON POLICE STATION   MISSING PERSONS

Name:
Sex:
Age:
Address:
Next of kin: type of clothing
Clothes—colour

1.
2.
3.
4.
5.

Other details:

SET 1   Describe people's appearance

What does she look like?	She's got fair hair.
What's she wearing?	She's wearing a grey coat.

1. Work in pairs. Use the police form to ask about Mandy's appearance like this:

What does she look like?
What's she wearing?
Are there any other important details?

Types of clothes

coat jacket trousers raincoat jeans
sweater shirt blouse tee-shirt
cardigan skirt dress shoes boots belt

Style of clothes

short-sleeved long-sleeved sleeveless

Hair styles

wavy curly straight a fringe

---

2. Match the words with the pictures, like this:

What does she look like?
She's got straight hair.
What's she wearing?
She's wearing a skirt and a short-sleeved shirt.

3. Work in pairs. Make notes to describe your partner, using the form.

Name:	Colour of hair:
Sex:	Hair style:
Occupation:	Colour of eyes:
Clothes: Colour	Type of clothing
1.	
2.	
3.	
4.	

4. Change partners. Ask and answer each other about your first partner, like this:

Has she/he got long hair?
Yes, that's right. Long brown hair.
Has she/he got green eyes?
No. Brown eyes.
Is he/she wearing a jersey?
Yes. A red jersey.
Is she/he wearing shoes?
No. Boots. Black boots.

SET 2 Ask about and narrate past actions

What time did you get up? I got up at 7.30.

POLICE REPORT FROM WITNESS

Missing person
Mandy Ingrams

Date: *25/9*

Name of witness: *Mrs Joan Ingrams*
51 Bath Road, Bristol

Relationship: *Mother of missing child*

Mrs I. – got up at 7.30. Had breakfast with family – husband and son, Mark, 4 years old. Daughter Mandy got ready for school, put on grey coat, said it was teacher's birthday, wanted to buy some flowers. Mrs I. gave her 20p. M. left house at 8.45. School is 5 minutes walk from house. Mrs I. has not seen her since then.

POLICE REPORT FROM WITNESS

Missing person
Mandy Ingrams

Date: *25/9*

Name of witness: *Mrs Marjorie Hawkins, The Sweet Shop, Central Parade, London Road, Bristol.*

Relationship: *None.*

Mrs. H. – owns sweet shop, Central Parade. Opened shop at 9. Little girl wearing grey coat came in. Red ribbon in hair. Girl had 20p. Girl asked, 'Do you sell flowers?' Mrs H. said 'No, I don't, but there are some pretty wild flowers near the canal.' Girl said, 'Thank you.'
Left shop at 9.10

---

1. **Work in pairs. You are the policeman, your partner is Mrs Ingrams. Use the notes in the Police Report to interview Mrs Ingrams. Ask questions like:**

What time did you get up?
What did you do then?
Did your husband take Mandy to school?
What did Mandy do then?
Did she say anything before she left?
Did you give her any money?
When did Mandy leave the house?
How far away is the school?
Have you seen her since?

useful verbs

get up/got up
have/had
leave/left
give/gave
put/put
want/wanted

2. **Work in pairs. You are the policeman, your partner is Mrs Hawkins. Use the notes in the Police Report to interview Mrs Hawkins. Ask questions like:**

What do you do?
What time did you open your shop this morning?
Did a little girl come into the shop?
What was she wearing?
How much money did she have?
What did she say?
What did you say?
Did she buy anything?
What time did she leave the shop?

useful verbs

open/opened
come/came
ask/asked

**POLICE REPORT
FROM WITNESS**

Missing person
Mandy Ingrams

Date: 25/9

Name of witness: Jack Priestman
5 Canal Lane, Bristol.

Relationship: None

Mr. P. — ....

3. Listen to the policeman interviewing another witness, Jack Priestman. Makes notes like those in the Police Reports for the other witnesses, Mrs Ingrams and Mrs Hawkins.

4. After interviewing the three witnesses, the policeman wrote out his notes in full. Read the report of his interview with Mrs Ingrams.

> Mrs Joan Ingrams who lives at 57, Bath Road, Bristol, is the
> mother of the missing child. On the morning of September 25th
> she got up at 7.30. Then she had breakfast with her family —
> her husband and her son, Mark. Then her daughter, Mandy, got
> ready for school. She put on her grey coat. Mandy said that
> she wanted to buy some flowers because it was her teacher's
> birthday. Mrs Ingrams gave Mandy 20p and Mandy left the house
> at 8.45. Mandy's school is about five minutes' walk from the
> house. Mrs Ingrams did not see her daughter again.

Write reports for the other two interviews.

On a police launch on the canal.

POLICEMAN: Have you found anything?

POLICEWOMAN: No, nothing. Have you checked with the station?

POLICEMAN: They haven't found anything either. Nobody has seen her. I think . . .

POLICEWOMAN: Wait a minute! Stop the engine. Look! Flowers! There are some flowers on the bank of the canal.

POLICEMAN: The woman in the sweetshop said something about flowers. You don't think . . .

POLICEWOMAN: Mandy saw some flowers and climbed down to pick them. Then she slipped and . . .

POLICEMAN: . . . fell in! It's possible. Poor little thing! Ah, here's the other launch. Any luck?

PATROLMAN: I don't know. We've just found this. It was floating in the water.

POLICEWOMAN: What is it?

PATROLMAN: Ribbon. It's a piece of red ribbon . . .

POLICEWOMAN: Oh, no!

POLICEMAN: You don't think she's . . .

POLICEWOMAN: Quick! Contact the police station. Tell them we need two divers and tell them it's urgent!

Why are the flowers important?
Because . . . .

Why is the red ribbon important?
Because Mrs Ingrams said that . . . .

Why do the police need two divers. *Because they think* . . . .

How do they think the accident happened?

 SET 3 Ask and talk about completed actions

Have you been to the cinema recently? No, I haven't.
Have you watched TV recently? Yes, I have.
What programmes did you watch? A football match and a detective film.

How do you spend your free time?
Think about the past few days . . .

Have you .... recently?	Yes	No	(if yes)
1 been to the cinema or theatre			What did you see? When?
2 watched TV			What did you watch?
3 read a book or part of a book			What was it about?
4 bought any books or records			What did you buy? Where?
5 bought any clothes			What did you buy? What are the clothes like?
6 been to a lecture or meeting			What was it about?
7 eaten out in a restaurant			Where did you go? What did you have?
8 invited any friends home			Who did you invite? What sort of occasion was it?
9 written a letter			Who did you write to?
10 done anything else interesting			What did you do?

1. **Work in pairs. Ask your partner about his/her recent activities, using the chart. Make notes of the answers. Ask like this:**

Have you been to the cinema recently?
Yes, I have.
What did you see?
I saw Star Wars.
etc.

2. **Tell the rest of the class what your partner has done, like this:**

Peter has done quite a lot of things in his spare time recently. He has been to the cinema to see Superman II and played a game of football. He has visited his cousins and has eaten out in a Pizzaria. He has also read a few chapters of a book about diamond smuggling.

3. **Write two paragraphs:**

1. about the things your partner has done recently.
2. about the things you have done recently.

Oral Exercises

1. Ask people about their taste in clothes

Barbara, do you like wearing dresses or jeans?
Oh, I like wearing jeans.

And do you like wearing tee-shirts or blouses?
Well, it depends.

Ask Barbara about:

1. dresses   jeans
2. tee-shirts   blouses
3. sweaters   cardigans

Ask Rod about:

1. trousers   jeans
2. short-sleeved shirts   long-sleeved shirts
3. boots   shoes

*2. Give your opinion about clothes and appearance. Say what *you* like.

Do you like long or short hair?
(Long hair—definitely.)

Do you like wearing tee-shirts?
(No, I don't, not at all.)

Do you like long or short hair?
Do you like wearing tee-shirts?
Do you like wearing jeans?
Do you like boots, sandals, or shoes?
What sort of hairstyle do you like?
What sort of clothes do you wear most of the time?

3. Apologise for not completing certain activities

The sergeant at Clifton Police Station is talking to one of the policemen.

Have you looked on the bank?
Not yet, I'm afraid. I'm just going to look there.

And have you talked to the woman in the sweetshop?
Not yet, I'm afraid. I'm just going to talk to her.

Have you looked on the bank?
And have you talked to the woman in the sweetshop?
Have you been to the school?
Have you spoken to Jack Priestman?
Well, have you rung Mandy's father?
And have you told Mrs Ingrams what's happening?

4. Say that you have completed certain activities

Two policemen are searching for Mandy.

What about looking on the bank?
I've just looked there.

How about talking to the woman in the sweetshop?
I've just talked to her.

What about looking on the bank?
How about talking to the woman in the sweetshop?
Shall we go to the school?
When are we going to speak to Jack Priestman?
We ought to ring Mandy's father.
And I think we've got to tell Mrs Ingrams what's happening.

5. Check details

You are with Barbara just before she leaves her flat to go to Italy. Check that she has done things.

Have you closed all the windows, Barbara?
Yes, I have. I've just done it.

Have you unplugged the TV?
Yes.

Check that Barbara has done these things on your list:

1. close all windows
2. unplug TV
3. turn off fridge
4. turn off lights
5. lock back door
6. cancel newspapers

Open Dialogue

Talk to Barbara.

BARBARA: Hi! How are you?
YOU: ....
BARBARA: What sort of week have you had?
YOU: ....
BARBARA: I've just come back from Italy.
YOU: ....
BARBARA: Have you been anywhere exciting this year?
YOU: ....
BARBARA: What about your next holidays? Where are you going?
YOU: ....
BARBARA: Have you ever been there before?
YOU: ....
BARBARA: Actually, I went to Italy on business—to buy some shoes.
Are you interested in shoes?
YOU: ....
BARBARA: Have you bought anything recently?
YOU: ....
BARBARA: Oh, well, why don't you come and see my boutique sometime?
See if you like my Italian shoes. Bye!

EXTENSION

EVENING BRISTOL GIRL IN CANAL DRAMA

by Mike Sanders

MANDY INGRAMS, a pretty fair-haired six-year-old girl, nearly drowned last Wednesday in the canal in Moss Park.

Mandy was on her way to school. It was her teacher's birthday and Mandy wanted to buy her some flowers. She went to the local sweet shop on Central Estate, but the owner, Mrs Marjorie Hawkins, told her that she did not sell flowers. So Mandy went to the bank of the canal in Moss Park to pick some wild flowers for her teacher.

UNCONSCIOUS

Three hours later, the police found Mandy. She was lying near the water and she was unconscious. She also had a broken leg. She was lying three inches from the edge of the canal. Police Constable Peggy Booth told me, 'Mandy is very lucky to be alive.' She had a very narrow escape.' Mandy is now in the children's ward at Bristol General Hospital.

NEXT TIME?

Once again, the Moss Park Canal is the scene of a near fatal accident. The canal passes very close to Saint John's First School. At this point it is over two metres deep. There are no fences. In fact, there is nothing to stop small children from falling into the water. It is time for the local authorities to do something about this dangerous playground. The next little Mandy may not be so lucky.

'AWARD' for t

1.

Why is the canal dangerous?
Because there aren't any .... and it is ....
Is there a dangerous 'playground' where you live?
Who do you think was responsible for what happened to Mandy?

2. Write the story of Mandy's accident from the time she left home in the morning until the time the police found her. Use:
   a) the dialogues and the pictures,
   b) the Police Reports from the witnesses,
   c) the newspaper article,
   to help you.
   Link events with *when* and *while*, like this:

When Mandy did not arrive at school, her teacher telephoned Mrs Ingrams.
While the police were searching, Mandy was lying unconscious near the edge of the canal.

The car won't start.	—check petrol
I have a terrible pain in my back.	—see doctor
I can't find my passport.	—look everywhere
I think there's a thief in the neighbourhood.	—tell police
Sally is having problems at school.	—talk to teacher
I can't get the TV to work.	—switch on

3. Work in pairs. Offer advice to your partner by checking if he/she has done things in these situations, like this:

   The car won't start.
   Have you checked the petrol?

4. Roleplay

   You arrive at London Airport. You are expecting a friend, Susan, to meet you at the arrival gate. She isn't there. So you wait half an hour and then telephone her. Susan's brother answers the telephone.

5. Listen to these people talking about their recent activities.

CHECK

Now you can:

1. Ask and talk about people's appearance

What does he look like?
He's got red hair.
What is she wearing?
She's wearing blue jeans.

2. Ask about and narrate past actions

What time did you get up?
I got up at 7.30.
What did you do then?
I had breakfast.

3. Ask and talk about completed actions

Have you been to the theatre recently?
No, I haven't, but I've been to the cinema.
Have you seen Star Wars?
Yes, I have. I've seen it twice.

Grammar

I've He's She's / We've You've They've	got	fair dark long short	hair.

I You We They	have('ve) haven't	finished the homework. watched TV this week. bought any oranges. written the letter.
He She	has('s) hasn't	

Have	you they	been to the theatre this week? played football recently? seen Star Wars?	Yes, No,	I they	have. haven't.
Has	he she			he she	has. hasn't.

Words and phrases

neighbours	jacket	boots	missing	lucky	decide	do our best
ribbon	trousers	sandals	calm	unconscious	expect	play truant
tights	raincoat	belt	short-sleeved	fatal	wear	narrow escape
skirt	fringe	witness	long-sleeved	urgent	slip	
sweater	jeans	canal	sleeveless		fall (fell)	
type	shirt	diver	wavy		contact	
appearance	blouse	edge	curly		drown	
style	cardigan	fence	straight			
	dress	launch	wild			

Pax Records
Press Release
LAURA DENNISON

1955	Born in Bristol
1960	Started school
1973	Went to Bristol University
1974	Joined a folk group
1975	Married Tony Harper
1976	Left university
1977	Won folk song competition
1978	Birth of daughter, Jody Recorded song 'The Price of Peace' (Number 3 in Top Twenty)
1979	American, South American and European tours. Went to live in Los Angeles.

Laura's new single 'Women are people too' is in your record shop NOW.

Mike Sanders interviews Laura Dennison, a folk singer, after a concert.

MIKE: That was a beautiful performance, Laura. And welcome back to Bristol.

LAURA: Thank you. Now, your questions. Oh, good, you've got my press release.

MIKE: Yes. You were born here in Bristol, weren't you, in 1955?

LAURA: That's right. I was born not far from this theatre, actually. But I grew up in the suburbs.

MIKE: And your parents?

LAURA: They came from Ireland originally. My father was a Customs Officer at the docks.

MIKE: Is he still there?

LAURA: No, he died about three years ago.

MIKE: Have you got any brothers or sisters?

LAURA: No, I'm an only child.

MIKE: Mmm. And then you went to university?

LAURA: Yes, for three years. That's where I wrote the song 'The Price of Peace'.

MIKE: And got married!

LAURA: Yes.

MIKE: How long have you been singing professionally?

LAURA: Oh, quite a long time! Actually, I've been singing *professionally* since 1978 when I recorded my first song.

MIKE: And now you're a world famous star, a composer and a mother. How do you manage to do it?

LAURA: Do what?

MIKE: Combine a career with a family?

LAURA: Are you married with a family, Mr Sanders?

MIKE: Yes, but . . .

LAURA: Well, do you find it difficult to be a journalist *and* a father?

MIKE: But . . .

LAURA: Think about it, Mr Sanders. Goodbye!

Did Laura grow up in the country? *No, she grew up ....*
....

What nationality were her parents? *They were ....*

What did her father do? *He was* ....

Is he still alive? ....

Does Laura come from a big family? ....

Where did she compose her first song? *When she was ....*

Where did Laura meet her husband?

Talk about events in people's lives

I was born *in* 1955.
He died three years *ago*.
I went to university *for* three years.
I have been singing professionally *since* 1978.

---

1. **Work in pairs. Ask and answer questions about Laura Dennison's life, using the press release.**

   a) **Use *in* with dates, like this:**

   When did Laura go to university?
   In 1976.

   When did she get married?
   When did she win the folk song competition?
   When did she tour South America?

   b) **Use *ago* with numbers of years; count back, like this:**

   When did Laura join the folk group?
   (If it is 1980 *now)* Six years ago.

   When did she leave university?
   When did she record her first song?
   When did she tour America?

   c) **Use *for* with numbers of years; count up, like this:**

   How long did Laura go to school for?
   For 13 years.

   How long did she go to university for?
   How long has she been married for?

   d) **Use *since* with dates, like this:**

   How long has Laura been singing?
   She has been singing since 1974.

   How long has she been singing professionally?
   How long has she been living in America?

2. **Work in pairs. Ask and answer these questions.**

   When did you first start school? *When I was* ....
   or *In* ....
   When did you leave school? .... *ago.* or *I haven't left yet.*
   How long did you stay at school? *or* How long have you been at school? *For* ...... *years.*
   How long have you been living in your present home? *I have been living there for/since* ....
   How long have you been studying at this school? *For/since* ....
   How long have you been learning English in this class? *For/since* ....
   How long have you been learning English with your present teacher? *For/since* ....
   How long have you been using this book? *For/since* ....

   Rod Nelson is Canadian He comes from Montreal. He is an engineer. At the moment he is living in Bristol in the south west of England. He has been living there for several months. He works in a small firm called Weston Aeronautics. He has been working there for four months.

   ---

3. **Read about Rod Nelson. Write a similar paragraph about a friend or relative. Say:**
   1. who they are
   2. what they do
   3. where they live
   4. how long they have been living there
   5. where they work/study
   6. how long they have been working/studying there.

SET 2   Ask and talk about people's background

Where were you born? I was born in Bristol.
Where did you grow up? I grew up in Bristol.
Where did you go to school? I went to a comprehensive school.
What did you do after that? I went to university.
  I went to work.
  I went abroad.

---

1. Complete this chart:

Background	I was born in .... (*place, country*)
Early life	I grew up in .... I went to school at .... for ....
Career	After studying at .... (*school*), I left and went to .... (*place of work, university, college*) to work/study.
Other information	I am an only child/I have got .... (*brothers/sisters, etc.*)

2. Work in pairs. Ask your partner about his/her past life. Make notes of his/her answers. Then make and complete a chart for your partner's life.

3.

Background to the STARS

LAURA DENNISON, famous singer and star of the Top Twenty, was born in Bristol. Her parents originally came from Ireland. Laura's father was a Customs Officer in the Bristol docks. Unfortunately, he died a few years ago.

Laura, who is an only child, grew up in the suburbs of Bristol. She started her education at a local school and then moved to a large, modern comprehensive school in another part of the city.

After leaving school when she was 18, Laura went to Bristol University for three years to study history and economics. While she was at university, Laura joined a university folk group and started singing. It was at this time that she wrote her famous song 'The Price of Peace'. Soon after finishing her university career, Laura joined another group and began to earn money with her performances and with her songs.

When she was 21, Laura was married to Tony Harper who was a student in the same year. Laura and Tony have two children—a daughter, Jody, and a son, Daniel. For several years the Harper family have been living in a beautiful farm house in the country outside Bristol, but recently they decided to leave Britain and move to Los Angeles.

4. There are four paragraphs in Mike Sanders' article. Which paragraph is about:

Laura's career? ......
Laura's background? ......
Other information about Laura? ......
Laura's early life? ......

5. Write a short autobiography (about yourself). Use Mike Sanders' article as a guide. Use your notes from Exercise 1.

Oral Exercises

1. Confirm dates

You are Laura Dennison. Mike Sanders is interviewing you. Look at the biographical details in the Press Release on page 105. Confirm dates of your past life.

You were born in the middle-fifties, weren't you?
Right. I was born in 1955.

And you went to university in the early seventies?
Right. I went to university in 1973.

You were born in the middle fifties, weren't you?
And you went to university in the early seventies?
You joined a folk group a year after, didn't you?
And you got married in the middle seventies?
Your daughter was born in the late seventies?
And you recorded a hit song in the same year?

2*. Talk about general points of time
Answer according to what *you* think.

When did you start these exercises?
Oh, (just a few minutes) ago.

When did you start using this book?
Oh, (a few months) ago.

When was the Second World War?
Oh, (a long time) ago.

When did you start these exercises?
When did you start using this book?
When was the Second World War?
When was the American Civil War?
When was your birthday?
When did you start school?

3. Ask how long people have been doing things

I live in Bristol.
Oh, how long have you been living there?

Rod works at Weston's now.
Oh, how long has he been working there?

I live in Bristol.
Rod works at Weston's now.
Paul and Sue both study at the Polytechnic.
We always go to Scotland for our holidays.
Barbara works near the new shopping centre.
My brother is studying in America.

4*. Say when and how long ago you did things
Answer according to *your* situation.

When did you first start studying here?
(Four years ago. In 1976.*)*

And how long have you been in this class?
(For two years. Since 1978.*)*

When did you first start studying here?
And how long have you been in this class?
When did you begin learning English?
And how long have you been using this book?
When did you last have a holiday?
And how long have you been working in your job?

5. Correct information about people's past lives
Read about Elvis Presley on page 111 before you do this exercise. Then correct the information.

Elvis was born in 1977.
No, that was when he died.

He died in 1935.
No, that was when he was born.

Elvis was born in 1977.
He died in 1935.
He won several talent competitions when he was a young man.
He met Colonel Parker when he was 30.
People criticised Elvis when he was middle-aged.

Open Dialogue
Talk to Mike Sanders about your past life.

MIKE: Hi! Do you mind if I talk to you?
YOU: ....
MIKE: Well, my questions are quite short. First, I'd like to know where you were born.
YOU: ....
MIKE: I see. And I suppose your parents were born in the same place.
YOU: ....
MIKE: Tell me something about them.
YOU: ....
MIKE: You've got some brothers and sisters, haven't you?
YOU: ....
MIKE: Mmm. Where did you first go to school?
YOU: ....
MIKE: Tell me something about your later education.
YOU: ....
MIKE: Do you mind if I ask you some questions about your private life?
YOU: ....
MIKE: Well, actually, I am in a bit of a hurry, so it doesn't matter. I'm afraid I've got to go.

EXTENSION

1. Mike Sander's notebook.

Notes for future articles on Bristol personalities

GERALDINE BEVAN – detective story writer

Background – born Edinburgh, Scotland 1938. Father novelist,
mother teacher. Parents from Wales originally.
Only child.

Early education – village school.

Later education – Edinburgh High School for Girls.

Early career – journalist in Edinburgh, later London.
Wrote first successful detective story at 20.

Later career – still writing successful books (all bestsellers)

Other information – won the 'Best Detective Story Writer of the
Year' award in 1977. Married – husband now
dead.

Note – Miss Bevan does not like talking about her private life.

IVOR JONES – boxer

Background – b. Swansea, South Wales, '55. Father miner, m. shop
assistant. Parents living. Middle child of 5
brothers.

Early education – Dock Street Junior School, Swansea.

Later education – Aberdale Comprehensive.

Early career – Left school at 15. Worked in docks.
Started boxing in youth club at 17.

Later career – Won light-weight championship – Olympic Gold Medal,
Montreal, '76. Became professional '78.

Other information – Married, 2 children, wife gymnastics teacher.
Going to leave Britain to live in Spain.

N.B. Ivor likes talking about his family.

2. Work in pairs. You are a newspaper reporter. Your partner is Geraldine Bevan or Ivor Jones. Interview her/him, using Mike Sanders' notes, like this:

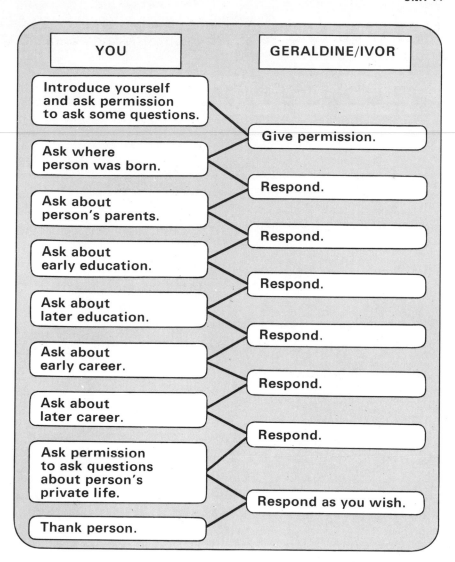

YOU	GERALDINE/IVOR
Introduce yourself and ask permission to ask some questions.	
	Give permission.
Ask where person was born.	
	Respond.
Ask about person's parents.	
	Respond.
Ask about early education.	
	Respond.
Ask about later education.	
	Respond.
Ask about early career.	
	Respond.
Ask about later career.	
	Respond.
Ask permission to ask questions about person's private life.	
	Respond as you wish.
Thank person.	

3. Listen to the Radio Bristol quiz 'Alive or Dead?' Try to guess the name of the person *before* the members of the quiz panel. Make notes:

> Is the person alive or dead?
> real or fictional?
> a man or a woman?
>
> What is his/her nationality?
> occupation?

Stop your tape and write down the answer if you think you have guessed it.

110

ELVIS PRESLEY

born January 8th 1935
died August 16th 1977

Elvis Aaron Presley was born on January 8 1935, in East Tupelo, Mississippi. His tw brother died at birth. Elvis grew up in a po but religious home which was typical of the deep south of the United States. His parent Vernon and Gladys Presley, were kind an loving.

While he was still a child, Elvis won sever talent competitions. Later, after he left schoo he worked as a cinema usher and a truc driver. This was the job Elvis always said h liked best.

The first person to realise that Elvis was a goo singer was Sam Phillips, the owner of a reco company called Sun Records. But the ma who really guided Elvis's career was Colon Tom Parker. Colonel Parker became Elvis manager in 1955 and soon made him into world famous rock and roll star.

By 1956, Elvis Presley had won six gold disc These were the first of many which he wo during his life. When he was young, Elvis ha many critics—particularly from the old generation. They thought that Elvis wa 'dangerous for the morals of young people Life—and people's attitudes—have change since 1956. And Elvis Presley helped change them.

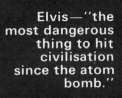

Elvis—"the most dangerous thing to hit civilisation since the atom bomb."

When and where was Elvis Presley born?

How old was he when he died?

Was he an only child?

How would you describe Elvis' early life—happy or unhappy?

What were Elvis' parents like?

How did he show his talent for singing?

When did he become really famous?

Who guided his career?

What did some parents say about young Elvis Presley?

Do you know the names of any Elvis Presley records?

What do you think about them?

Which modern singers and entertainers do you like?

CHECK

Now you can:

1. Ask about the past	When was he born? How long did you go to school for? How long has she been singing professionally?
2. Talk about the past	He was born in 1935. He was born 45 years ago. I went to school for seven years. She's been singing professionally for three years. She's been singing professionally since 1978.
3. Ask about people's past lives	Where were you born? Where did you go to school? What did you do after that?
4. Talk about your past life and other people's past lives	I was born in Cardiff. He went to school in Cardiff. She left school and went to work.

Grammar

When Where	were you		born?
	was	he she	

I He She	was born	in 1958. twenty years ago. in Cardiff.

I We You They	have	been living in Cardiff	since 1965. for 14 years.
He She	has		

Words and phrases

star (pop star)	competition	gymnastics	fictional	record a song
folk singer	comprehensive school	talent		combine
song	background	Top Twenty		tour
group	history	successful	originally	go abroad
customs officer	economics	lightweight	ago	earn
docks	detective	loving	since	realise
hit	novelist	religious		guide
peace	bestseller	alive		change
composer	miner	dead/died	be born	manage
		real	grow up	sing
			get married	begin

UNIT 15
AND TOMORROW...?

Jack Cooper decided to apply for a job in the first European branch of Weston Aeronautics in Toulouse in France.

His application was successful and the company made all the travel arrangements for the Coopers to go to France. One morning Jack received a letter with the details of the travel arrangements.

Weston Aeronautics
Avon Trading Estate, Jubilee Drive, BRISTOL 9

Tuesday July 15th

Dear Mr and Mrs Cooper,

<u>Toulouse - travel arrangements</u>

I enclose details of your travel arrangements for your journey to Toulouse on Saturday 19th July, for you and your wife.

A company car will arrive at your house at 8 a.m. to take you to the airport. The driver will have your tickets. Please make sure that you have your passports.

The plane leaves at 9.30 a.m. and check-in time is at 8.30. Your baggage allowance is 20 kilos each. The flight to Toulouse will take an hour and a half. Breakfast will be served during the flight.

There will be a representative of the company at the arrival gate to meet you at Toulouse. He will have a card saying 'Mr and Mrs J. Cooper - Weston Aeronautics'. He will take you to your hotel in the city centre. He will have some French currency for your immediate use.

I hope these arrangements are satisfactory and that you both have a pleasant journey.

Yours sincerely,

Freda Curtis

Freda Curtis
Personnel Officer

Ask and talk about travel arrangements

| How will we get to the airport? | A car will pick us up at 8 a.m. |

1. **Jack and Peggy discussed the journey to France. Complete their conversation, using the information in the letter.**

PEGGY: Has the Personnel Officer sent all our travel arrangements for the 19th?

JACK: ....

PEGGY: Then everything is all right, isn't it?

JACK ....

PEGGY: Well, then, how will we get to the airport?

JACK: ....

PEGGY: But what about the tickets? They haven't sent them—why?

JACK: ....

PEGGY: Oh. I hope he doesn't forget them! 8 o'clock is very early. Will we get anything to eat during the flight?

JACK: ....

PEGGY: Oh, that's good. But what about when we get to the other end—in Toulouse? Will anyone meet us?

JACK: ....

PEGGY: Well, that sounds all right. What about money? We haven't got any French francs yet.

JACK: ....

PEGGY: Fine. And where are we going to stay?

JACK: ....

PEGGY: Lovely! I'm looking forward to that. By the way, Jack, how will the person meeting us know who we are?

JACK: ....

PEGGY: Well, everything is arranged, then. I don't know why you are getting so worried, Jack!

2. Work in pairs. Read the conversation.

3. Listen to Jack and Peggy talking about their travel arrangements to France. Look at the conversation in Exercise 1. (Notice that it is different, but the information is the same.)

TRAVEL ARRANGEMENT ALTERNATIVES

	Alternatives
1. Transport to airport	airport bus taxi company car lift from a friend
2. Food during flight	breakfast lunch dinner light snack juice/tea/coffee
3. Arrival and meeting arrangements	travel courier/special bus company representative/company car my parents/car nobody/airport bus
4. First night accommodation	hotel in city centre my parents' house with friends on the night train to (Milan)

4. Work in pairs. Talk about travel arrangements using the chart.
Ask and answer like this:

1. How will we get to the airport?
   We'll take the airport bus. *or*
   A friend will give us a lift.

2. Will we get anything to eat during the flight?
   Yes, we'll get .... *or*
   No, we'll only get ....

3. Who will meet us when we arrive?
   A travel courier will meet us with a special bus.

4. Where will we spend the first night?
   We'll spend it at/in/on/with ....

Friday 18th July, at the Coopers' house.

PEGGY: Get the glasses out, Jack. They'll be here soon.

JACK: You know, Peggy, I don't think Rod will come. They've had another row.

PEGGY: Nonsense! It was only a little row! I'm quite sure he'll come to say goodbye to us.

(Doorbell rings. Jack opens the door.)

BARBARA: Hi!

JACK: You're alone, are you!

BARBARA: Yes.

JACK: Where's Rod?

PEGGY: Please, Jack—

BARBARA: Oh, he's getting some wine from the off-licence. He won't be a moment. Just think, mum! By this time tomorrow, you'll both be in France!

PEGGY: Yes. Oh dear! I'll miss all my friends.

BARBARA: No, you won't. I'm sure you won't. Well, only for a bit.

JACK: I think we'll be very happy.

(Doorbell rings.)

BARBARA: That'll be Rod. Don't bother, I'll open the door.

ROD: Hello, Mrs Cooper. Hi, Jack! Excited about your journey?

PEGGY: Yes, very.

ROD: But what about the language, Mrs Cooper?

PEGGY: Well, I don't know—

JACK: Oh, she'll be all right. Peggy took evening classes in French.

PEGGY: I didn't learn much. We did grammar all the time. We didn't learn how to *speak* the language.

ROD: Don't worry! It won't be very difficult once you get there.

PEGGY: Perhaps you're right.

ROD: Right! The wine—sparkling French wine! Cheers!

BARBARA: What do they say in France?

ROD: Salut!

JACK: We say 'Cheers!'

BARBARA: Cheers, mum! Cheers, dad! I hope you'll both be very, very happy.

ROD: Good luck!

PEGGY: Thank you, Rod. And you will come to see us, won't you? Both of you.

BARBARA: I'm sure it will be soon, won't it, Rod?

Why are the Coopers celebrating?

Why doesn't Jack think Rod will come?

Why is Barbara 'alone'?

Does Barbara think that her mother will be unhappy in France?

Where did Peggy learn French?

Why didn't she learn much?

How does Peggy show that she likes Rod?

In Britain people often say 'Cheers!' when they drink. What do you say?

What do you think is going to happen to Rod and Barbara?

SET 2 Make and comment on predictions

I'll miss all my friends. No, you won't.
I'm sure you won't.

I think we'll be very happy.

Make a prediction	*Agree positively*	*Agree neutrally*	*Disagree*
I think Barbara will marry Rod.	Yes, I'm sure she will. Yes, so do I. Yes, I do, too.	Well, maybe she will. Mmm, possibly. Perhaps.	No, she won't! Do you? I don't. Well, I don't think she will.
I don't think Barbara will marry Rod.	No, I'm sure she won't. Neither do I. Nor do I. I don't either.	Well, maybe she won't. Mmm, possibly not. Perhaps not.	Yes, she will! Don't you? I do. Well, I think she will.

Predictions

I think I'm sure I don't think	Barbara will	marry Rod. be very successful. change her job. marry someone else.	
	Rod will	go back to Canada. stay in Britain. go to the U.S.A. marry Barbara.	
	the Coopers will	like France. come home soon. miss England. make a lot of friends.	
	the weather tomorrow will be	fine. hot. cold. wet.	

1. **Work in pairs. Make positive predictions and comment on them as you want, like this:**
   I think Barbara will marry Rod.
   Well, maybe she will.

2. **Make negative predictions and comment on them as you want, like this:**
   I don't think Barbara will marry Rod.
   No, I'm sure she won't.

3. **Write out 3 more predictions about the people in the book. Tell the other people in your group your predictions and comment on other people's predictions.**

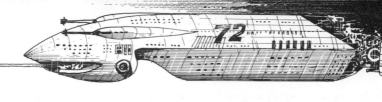

LIFE IN THE 21ST CENTURY

WHAT WILL IT BE LIKE?

What do you think will happen in the future? Say what you think about these different topics.

	AGREE	NEUTRAL	DISAGREE
1 Life style			
Everyone will live in cities.			
There will be houses under the sea.			
Families will live in communes.			
Marriage will be out of date.			
People will live on the moon.			
Every house will have a video telephone.			
Houses and factories will use solar energy.			
2 Education			
Children will start school at 3.			
Computers will replace teachers.			
People will study until they are 30.			
3 Work			
People will only work 4 hours a day.			
People will stop work at 45.			
All factories and offices will be run by cooperatives.			
4 Politics			
America will have a woman President.			
Britain will have a black Prime Minister.			
There will be a law against having more than two children.			
China will be under Russian control.			
There will be a law against keeping pets.			
All atomic weapons will be destroyed.			
5 Transport and travel			
....			
....			
....			

4. Complete and fill in the questionnaire. Work in pairs or groups. Tell other people your predictions and comment on their predictions, like this:

I think that in the future everyone will live in cities. Do you?
Yes, I do, too. *or*
I don't think they will.

5. Write some of your predictions about what life will be like in the 21st century. Use your answers to the questionnaire and this guide:

Life in the Twenty-first Century

Paragraph 1:
Introduction
Life in the 21st century will obviously be very different from what life is like today. It is interesting to try to predict what life will be like in the future.

Paragraph 2:
Life style
Our life style will be different in many ways. For example, I think that ....

Paragraph 3:
Education
As for education in the future, I think ....

Paragraph 4:
Work
Our working life will be different in many ways too. It is possible that ....

Paragraph 5:
Politics
I am sure that there will be political changes. I think ....

Paragraph 6:
Transport and Travel
Finally, when we think about the future of transport and travel, it seems to me that it is quite possible that ....

117

Talk about language and cultural differences

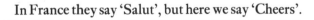

In France they say 'Salut', but here we say 'Cheers'.

British English	American English
petrol	drapes
lift	faucet
taxi	railroad
railway	gasoline
tap	fall
autumn	sidewalk
chips	cab
pavement	pants
trousers	French fries
curtains	chips
crisps	elevator

1. **Match the word in British English with the word in American English that means the same thing, like this:**
   In Britain they say 'petrol', but in America they say 'gasoline'.

Country	How they say goodbye
Britain	Auf wiedersehen
Germany	So long
France	Arrivederci
Italy	Adios
Mexico	Sayonara
America	Au revoir
Japan	Goodbye

2. **Match the countries with how people say goodbye. Compare different ways of saying goodbye, like this:**
   In Britain they say 'Goodbye', but in France they say 'Au revoir'.

3. **Find differences between your country and Britain. Think about:**
   festivals and national celebrations
   customs and social behaviour
   national regulations.

Oral Exercises

1. Confirm travel arrangements (1)

Will anyone meet us at the airport?
Yes, there'll be someone.

Will we get a meal on the plane?
Yes, there'll be a meal.

Will anyone meet us at the airport?
Will we get a meal on the plane?
Will we get a bus to the hotel?
Will there be anyone to meet us at the hotel?
Will we get any lunch at the hotel?
Will we have a bath in our hotel room?

2. Confirm travel arrangements (2)
You are Freda Curtis, the Personnel Officer at Weston's. Jack Cooper rings you about his trip. Use the information in the letter on page 113 to answer him.

Good morning, Mrs Curtis. I'm ringing about the trip to Toulouse. Will we have to order a taxi to the airport?
No, you won't.

And what about the check-in time? Will we have to be there by 8.30?
Yes, you will.

Will we have to order a taxi to the airport?
And what about the check-in time? Will we have to be there by 8.30?
Then baggage. Will we be able to have more than 20 kilos each?
Oh, and will we get anything to eat on the plane?
But when we get to France, will we have a hotel?
Yes, but will we have to find the hotel ourselves?
I see. And will we get any French money?

3. Agree with predictions (1)

I don't think Rod will stay at Weston.
Nor do I.

I think he'll go back to Canada.
So do I.

I don't think Rod will stay at Weston.
I think he'll go back to Canada.
Because I think Barbara's too independent for him.
You see, I don't think she'll stay in Bristol.
I think she'll move to London and open a shoe shop there.
So I don't think Rod will want to stay in Bristol.

4. Agree with predictions (2)

I think Jack Cooper will enjoy the job in France.
Yes, I do, too.

But I don't think Peggy will find it so easy there.
No, I don't either.

I think Jack Cooper will enjoy the job in France.
But I don't think Peggy will find it so easy there.
I think she'll miss her friends a bit.
But I think she'll learn French quite quickly.
But I don't think Jack will.
Because I think he'll speak English most of the time at work.

5.* Agree or disagree with predictions
Agree or disagree as *you* wish.

Now take Barbara, for example. She's pretty, she's clever and she's got a good job. I think she'll be very successful.
(Yes, so do I.)

I think she'll soon move to London.
(Oh, I don't think she will.)

I think Barbara will be successful.
I think she'll soon move to London.
And I think she'll never marry Rod.
I think she'll soon get settled down and be a housewife.
I don't think she'll combine her career and a family.
I think she'll be very content just to be a mother.

6. Question people's predictions
A friend is talking about a day trip to a seaside town.

I think it'll be fine tomorrow.
Oh? Do you really think it will?

Yes, so there'll be a lot of traffic on the roads.
Oh? Do you really think there will?

And there won't be anywhere to park in Bournemouth.
Oh, do you really think think there won't?

I think it'll be fine tomorrow.
Yes, so there'll be a lot of traffic on the roads.
And there won't be anywhere to park in Bournemouth.
I think the beach will be awful.
Yes, because there'll be so many people.
And there won't be any place to sit down.
Or else there'll be a lot of oil on the beach.
Look, let's stay at home. It'll be much nicer . . .

EXTENSION

1. Work in groups. A group of Australian teen-agers are coming to stay in your town for two weeks, to get to know the people and learn the language. Plan all the arrangements for them.

   Discuss them like this:

Meeting and arrival	We will meet the party at ...... on ....
Transport to their accommodation	A coach will ....
Accommodation	They will stay in/at/with ....
Language classes	They will go to classes at ....
Freetime activities	There will be some/a ...... at/in ...... on ....
Return journey	They will travel by ...... to ...... at ...... on ....
Other details	....

2. Write a letter to the leader of the group, giving details of the arrangements. Use the letter on page 113 as a guide. Start like this:

   Dear Miss Fountain,
   Here are the arrangements for the group which is coming to stay in ...... for two weeks.

3. Work in groups. Find out if anyone in the group is planning to go on a journey in the near future. If they are, ask them to tell you about their travel arrangements.

4. Listen to the report of an American dip-lomat's world tour. As you listen:

   a) trace his route from Washington,
   b) note the name of each city he will stop at,
   c) note the date of each stop,
   d) note the topics he will discuss—note the number from this list:

   1 Food production   4 Sino-Indian relations
   2 South East Asia   5 The space programme.
   3 Oil and pollution

5.

IN THE YEAR 2001

In the home, cookers will be set so that you can cook a complete meal at the touch of a switch.

Television will provide information on prices at the nearby shops as well as news and entertainment. Videophones will bring pictures as well as sound to telephone conversations.

Machines will control temperature, lighting, entertainment, security alarms, laundry and gardening.

Lighting will provide decoration as well as wallpaper.

At work, robots will take over most jobs in the manufacturing industries. Working hours will fall to under 30 hours a week. Holidays will get longer. Six weeks will be the normal annual holiday. Men and women will retire at the same age.

Our leisure will be different too. The home will become the centre of entertainment through television and electronic games. More people will eat out in restaurants than they do today; also they will have a much wider variety of food available. In Britain, there will be a change of taste towards a more savoury-flavoured menu. New synthetic foods will form a regular part of people's diets.

Foreign travel will increase; winter holidays will become more popular than summer ones. Also non-stop flights from Britain to Australia and New Zealand will be cheap and easily available. Hobbies and education will become increasingly important.

6. Work in pairs. Read the article on Life in 2001 and count the number of predictions for each topic:

Topic	Number of predictions
Home	......
Work	......
Leisure	......

CHECK

Now you can:

1. Ask about travel arrangements	How will we get to the airport? Who will meet us?
2. Talk about travel arrangements	A representative will be at the airport to meet you. The flight will take an hour.
3. Make predictions	I think Barbara will marry Rod. I don't think Barbara will marry Rod. There will be a law against pets. Everyone will live in cities. That'll be Rod at the door.
4. Agree positively with predictions	Yes, I'm sure she will./Yes, so do I./Yes, I do, too. No, I'm sure she won't./I don't, either./Neither do I./Nor do I.
5. Disagree with predictions	No, she won't./Yes, she will./Well, I don't think she will. Don't you? I do./Do you? I don't./Well, I think she will/won't.
6. Agree neutrally with predictions	Well, maybe she will./Mmm, possibly (not). Well, maybe she won't./Perhaps (not).
7. Talk about language and cultural differences	In France they say 'Salut', but here we say 'Cheers'.

Grammar

I You He She We They	will('ll) will not(won't)	be happy. go to France.

Will Won't	I you he she we they	be happy? go to France?

Yes,	she he	will.
No,		won't.

There's There was There will be	someone at the airport.

It's	a lovely day.
It'll	rain tomorrow.
It'll	be fine next week.

That's right.   That was a beautiful performance.   That'll be Rod.

I don't, either = Neither do I = Nor do I.   I do, too = So do I.

Words and phrases

application	franc	video	excited	neutrally	receive
arrangements	juice	energy	positive	neither	make sure
personnel officer	snack	pets	bored	nor	celebrate
baggage allowance	row	weapons	engaged	either	care
representative	off-licence	tap	atomic	maybe	enclose
currency	commune	pavement	solar		Don't bother
use	moon	immediate		apply	Nonsense!

1. Roleplay

Work in pairs. You are Mike Sanders; your partner is Rod Nelson. Interview Rod, using information from the book and your imagination. Use these ideas to help to prepare your interview:

When/where born
Where grew up/lived as a child
Family background—parents/brothers/sisters
Education—where/how long ago
Early career—where/first job
How long?—as electrical engineer
               living in Bristol
               intends to stay in Britain
Interests
Recent activities—what places visited/what seen/what done
Opinions—Bristol/English food/English people
Comparisons with Canada
Predictions for future—job/life in five years' time.

2. Discussion

Work in groups. Discuss the best way to travel. Use these questions to help you start your discussion:

Have you ever travelled by plane?
Where to?
Did you enjoy it?
Did anything go wrong?
Was it better/worse than other means of transport? Why?
Which way of travelling is most comfortable? most convenient? cheapest? most inconvenient? Why?
Have you ever had any dramatic/exciting/amusing/unusual experiences when travelling?
Is travelling becoming easier or more difficult? Why?
What will travel be like in the year 2002?

3. Open Dialogue

Talk to Barbara. You meet at the check-in desk at London Airport.

BARBARA: Hello, there! What a surprise! How are you?
YOU: ....
BARBARA: Anyway, what are you doing here?
YOU: ....
BARBARA: Really! Well. I'm just off to Canada. Ottawa, actually. Have you ever been there?
YOU: ....
BARBARA: Oh. Well, I'm opening a shoe boutique there.
YOU: ....
BARBARA: Of course, you haven't heard my news.
YOU: ....
BARBARA: Well, I've got engaged. Yes! I think I'll be happy over there.
YOU: ....
BARBARA: Where do you think you'll be this time next year?
YOU: ....
BARBARA: Well, be good, won't you? Whatever you do.
YOU: ....
BARBARA: And your English is so good now. You will work hard at it, won't you?
YOU: ....
BARBARA: Well, it was nice meeting you again. Bye!
YOU: ....

4. Jack Cooper

Complete the text about Jack Cooper. Put the verbs in the brackets ( ) in their right form.

Jack Cooper (be) production manager at Weston Aeronautics for ten years. He (live) in a small house in the suburbs of Bristol with his wife, Peggy. At the moment, Weston (expand) into Europe and they (build) a new factory in Toulouse.

A few months ago, Jack (go) to Toulouse to look at the new factory. He (talk) to Peter Chester, managing director of Weston about the new jobs there.

Jack (like) the sound of the new jobs and (think) that he would like to work in France. When he (get) back to Bristol, he (discuss) things with his wife. But they (decide) to wait for a time before making a decision to leave Bristol.

They (discuss) whether to go or not for two weeks now, but they (not make) up their minds yet.

The cost of living (be) higher in France, but Weston say they (provide) a house with the job—so in fact, the money Jack (earn) in Toulouse (be) better than in Bristol.

5. Fill in the correct prepositions.

1. I don't go ...... work ...... Saturdays or Sundays.
2. We arrived ...... London ...... exactly eight o'clock.
3. Come ...... ten o'clock ...... Friday morning.
4. He was born ...... five ...... the morning ...... December 25th.
5. He died ...... 1934.
6. The coffee is ...... the blue cupboard ...... the top shelf.
7. We went ...... London ...... car.
8. Get ...... the number 33 bus and get off ...... the third stop.
9. Who is John talking ......? I don't recognise her.
10. What are they talking ......?
11. Thanks ...... the lovely flowers.
12. The bus stop is ...... the bottom ...... the road.
13. Walk ...... this road and turn left ...... the traffic lights.
14. Thanks, and the same ...... you.
15. I must write ...... my mother.
16. I stayed ...... school ...... the age of 16.
17. I started work ...... 17.
18. I'm staying ...... friends.
19. ...... dinner, I like listening ...... records.
20. Let's go ...... a walk ...... the garden.
21. They have lived ...... the same house ...... ten years.
22. They got married 5 years ....
23. He's been sitting ...... the library ...... ten o'clock this morning.
24. ...... breakfast, she washed up and made the beds.

6. Complete these conversational exchanges.

1. A: ....
   B: Greece? No, never. Have you?
2. A: ....
   B: No, I haven't. I thought washing the car was your job.
3. A: ....
   B: I thought it was marvellous. I don't often go to concerts so I was quite surprised.
4. A: Why do you think a Volvo is better than a Jaguar?
   B: ....
5. A: I thought you had a job in the record shop after leaving college.
   B: ....
   A: Oh, I see. I don't know how you can study and work at the same time.
6. A: ....
   B: Ten years! I don't think I'd like to work in the same place for ten years.
7. A: When did you leave school?
   B: ....
   A: Was it so long ago? What have you been doing for the past ten years, then?
8. A: ....
   B: Since 1975. We moved from the London flat in November of 1975.
9. A: ....
   B: In 1945. He was the youngest of a family of five.
10. A: ....
    B: No, I haven't. I'm an only child.
11. A: How will you get to your parents' house from the airport?
    B: ....
    A: Oh, that's kind of them. I didn't realise they had a car.
12. A: What do you think of Brazil's chances in the world cup?
    B: ....
    A: So do I. They've got a very good team and a fantastic goalkeeper.

7. The Landlady

adapted from a short story by Roald Dahl.

'Mr Mulholland liked a cup of tea,' she said. 'I have never seen anyone drink as much tea as dear, sweet Mr Mulholland. Never in my life.'

'I suppose he left quite recently,' Billy said. He was still thinking about the two names. He was sure he had seen them in the newspapers.

5 'Left?' she said, surprised. 'But my dear boy, he never left. He's still here. Mr Temple is also here. They're on the third floor together.'

Billy put down his cup slowly on the table and stared at his landlady. She smiled at him, and then she put out one of her white hands and patted him on his knee. 'How old are you, my dear?' she asked.

10 'Seventeen.'

'Seventeen!' she cried. 'Oh, it's a perfect age! Mr Mulholland was also seventeen. But I think he was shorter than you are, and his teeth weren't quite so white. You have the most beautiful teeth, Mr Weaver, did you know that?'

15 'They're not as good as they look,' Billy said.

'Mr Temple, of course, was a little older,' she said. 'He was actually twenty-eight. But he didn't look twenty-eight. There wasn't a blemish on his body.'

'A what?' Billy said.

20 'A mark, my dear, there wasn't a mark. His skin was just like a baby's.'

Billy picked up his teacup and took another sip of his tea. He waited for her to say something else, but she was silent. He sat and stared into the far corner of the room, biting his lower lip.

'That parrot,' he said at last. 'You know something? When I first saw
25 it, I thought it was alive.'

'Alas, no longer.'

'It's terribly clever,' he said. 'It doesn't look the least bit dead. Who did it?'

'I did.'

30 'You did?'

'Of course,' she said. 'And have you met my little Basil as well?'

She nodded towards the dachshund in front of the fire.

Billy looked at it. He put out his hand and touched it on top of its back. It was cold and hard.

35 'Good gracious me!' he said. 'How absolutely fascinating! It must be awfully difficult to do a thing like that.'

'Not in the least,' she said. 'I stuff *all* my little pets myself when they die. Would you like another cup of tea?'

'No, thank you,' Billy said. The tea tasted strange—faintly of bitter
40 almonds—and he didn't like it very much.

'You signed the book, didn't you?'

'Oh, yes.'

'That's good. Because later on, if I forget your name, then I can come down here and look it up. I still do that almost every day with Mr
45 Mulholland and Mr . . . Mr . . .'

'Temple,' Billy said. 'Gregory Temple. Excuse me asking, but haven't there been any other guests here except them in the last two or three years?'

Holding her teacup high in one hand, she looked at him and gave
50 another gentle little smile.

'No, my dear,' she said. 'Only you!'

8. **Listen to a reading of 'The Landlady' from the radio series 'Stories after midnight'. Follow the text.**

9. **Acting**
   Work in pairs. Use the dialogue of the story to act the scene between the landlady and Billy Weaver.

10. **Text study**
    In the story there are many pronouns like *'them', 'he', 'it', 'they',* and *'that'*. Study the text and say what these pronouns refer to. Like this:

    1. *them* line 4 refers to *the two names*

    1. *them* line 4
    2. *he*   5
    3. *it*   11
    4. *they*   15
    5. *it*   25
    6. *it*   28
    7. *it*   34
    8. *that*   36
    9. *it*   40
    10. *it*   44
    11. *that*   44

11. **Work in pairs or small groups. Discuss these questions about the story 'The Landlady'.**

    1. Why do you think that the 'two names' had been in the newspaper?
    2. The landlady thought that Billy and the other two people were attractive. What did she like about them?
    3. Why do you think there have been no other guests in the house since Mr Mulholland and Mr Temple?
    4. What is the landlady's special skill?
    5. What do you think is going to happen to Billy?
    6. What do you think you would find upstairs in the house?
    7. Would you go upstairs?

12. Listen to the commentary from a fashion show. The commentator will say the name of each model and describe his/her clothes. Write the names of each model by each picture.

13. Use the Transit Tours notes to write a letter to Mike Sanders, giving details of the arrangements for his trip to New York. Use the letter on page 113 as a guide.

TRANSIT TOURS	**Travel Arrangements**	
	Name of client:	Mr. M. Sanders
	Address:	36, River Drive, Bristol 6.
	Destination:	New York (Kennedy Airport)
	Date:	August 16th
	Airport:	Heathrow
	Flight time:	1300
	Transport to airport:	Bus from terminal 1130
	Check-in time:	1200
	Arrival:	Travel courier will meet Bristol party

14. Famous Lives

Marie Curie Physicist French 1867–1934
Marie Curie, who was a famous French physicist, was born in 1867 and died in 1934.

Write similar sentences about two of these famous people:

Luigi Pirandello Playwright Italian
1867–1937
John D. Rockefeller Oil Tycoon American
1839–1937
Anna Pavlova Ballerina Russian 1885–1931

Now find out about two famous people from your country and write about them.

15. Quiz

Make two groups: Team A and Team B.
Take turns to answer the questions.
Listen to the instructions on the tape.
Stop the tape after each question.
You will hear the right answer before you hear the next question.
See which team answers most questions correctly.

16. Game: Alibi

Work in groups of 4 or 5.

Last night two people broke into the local bank. The police think that you and your partner are the thieves. You and your partner make up a story together to explain what you both did between 6 and 9 p.m. last night (you were together at the time). Your story is your 'alibi'. The others in your group ask you questions—first to you, then to your partner—to see if your stories are the same. If they are, you are innocent. If they are not, you are guilty!

RULES

1. You need: a dice, counters and 2, 3 or 4 players.
2. Each player chooses an airline with a flight number to begin the journey to Paradise Island.
   These are:
   British Airways—Flight BA 806
   Varig (Brazilian Airlines)—Flight VA 578
   Scandinavian Airlines System—Flight SK 432
   Japan Airlines—Flight JL 143
3. Each player starts from a different airport on the board and moves clockwise round the board until he lands on the correct. Flight Path to Paradise Island.
4. At each stopover the player reads the Flight Report for that stopover. He/She must do two things:
   a) carry out a language function
   b) read and obey the flight instruction.
5. A player must throw the correct number to land safely on the island. The first player to reach Paradise Island is the winner. The other players can continue the game for second and third positions.
6. To start the flight, all players throw the dice once. The player with the highest number starts.

Are you ready?

Have you chosen your airport and airline?

Have you checked your flight number?

Turn over, and have a good journey!

Flight to Paradise Island
a game of chance and language strategies

INTERNATIONAL FLIGHT REPORT

Accra: Arrange to meet the player on your right on Paradise Island. Telephone and describe what you look like. *Fly direct to Nairobi.*

Athens: Tell the player on your left why you think your airline is better. *Get on the wrong plane and go to Nandi.*

Auckland: You need to change some money. Ask about a bank. *Go back to Honolulu.*

Baghdad: Ask the air attendant for a newspaper. Name the one you would like. *Miss a turn.*

Bangkok: You've lost your suitcase. Tell the player on your right what it's like and what's in it. *Go back to Tokyo.*

Bogota: You have a headache and feel sick. Ask the air attendant for help. *Miss a turn.*

Brazilia: You forgot to close your window at home. Telephone a neighbour (player on your left) and ask for help. *You are re-routed to Honolulu.*

Budapest: Tell all the players what the weather is like today. *Fly direct to Tokyo.*

Cairo: You visit the Pyramids and lose your passport. Tell the police what happened. *Throw 6 to land on Paradise Island.*

Calcutta: Make two predictions about your future life on Paradise Island. *Fly to Ho Chi Minh City.*

Caracas: You stay at the Caracas Hilton. Ask about the facilities in the hotel. *You are re-routed to Vienna.*

Casablanca: Tell the other players about three things you did in the last place you visited. *You are re-routed to Brazilia.*

Columbo: Ask the player opposite you if he/she knows which country you are in. *If he/she knows, have another turn. If he/she doesn't know, go back to Nandi.*

Dar-es-Salaam: Ask about the beaches on Paradise Island. *Throw 6 to land.*

Djakarta: Ask any player a question about his/her background. *Miss a turn.*

Ho Chi Minh City: Describe where you live to the passenger (player) on your left. *Fly back to Peking to the World Table-Tennis Championship.*

Honolulu: Ask the player on your left where he/she has come from. *Invite him/her to join you in Honolulu and continue his/her journey from there.*

Kingston: Talk to the player opposite you. Suggest some things to do in your capital city. *Invite him/her to join you in Kingston and continue his/her journey from there.*

London: Flight BA 806 starts here.

Melbourne: Ask the passenger on your left if he/she would like a drink and ask the air attendant for drinks for both of you. *Miss a turn.*

Montreal: Ask the air attendant for a seat in the non-smoking part of the plane. *Fly direct to Honolulu.*

Nairobi: You photograph the wild animals. Tell the other players what equipment you have brought. *Miss a turn.*

Nandi: You go swimming and see a shark near the beach. Warn people of the danger. *Go back to Vancouver.*

Paris: You spill a drink on the passenger next to you. Apologise and offer help. *You are re-routed to Brazilia.*

Peking: You visit the Great Wall of China. Tell the other players your opinion of it. *Ask the player opposite to join you in Peking and continue his/her journey from there.*

Perth: An Australian friend has invited you to visit him. Telephone him, refuse his invitation and give an excuse. *Go back to Singapore.*

Rio de Janeiro: Flight VA 578 starts here.

Rome: The aircrew are leaving. Thank them and say goodbye. *Fly direct to Budapest.*

Singapore: Telephone all the other players and tell them about the last place you visited and what you did there. *Ask them all to join you in Singapore.*

Stockholm: Flight SK 432 starts here.

Tokyo: Flight JL 143 starts here.

Vancouver: You don't like your seat. Ask the air attendant if you can change it. *You are re-routed to Tokyo.*

Vienna: Ask the player opposite if he/she knows how to say 'Thank you' in German. *If he/she knows, you have another turn. If he/she doesn't know, miss a turn.*

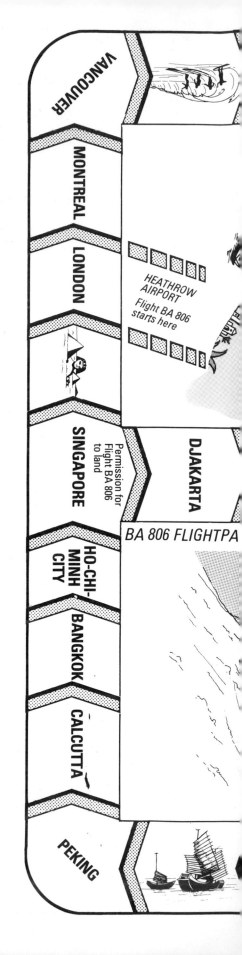

VANCOUVER

MONTREAL

LONDON

HEATHROW AIRPORT
Flight BA 806 starts here

SINGAPORE

Permission for Flight BA 806 to land

DJAKARTA

BA 806 FLIGHTPA

HO-CHI-MINH CITY

BANGKOK

CALCUTTA

PEKING

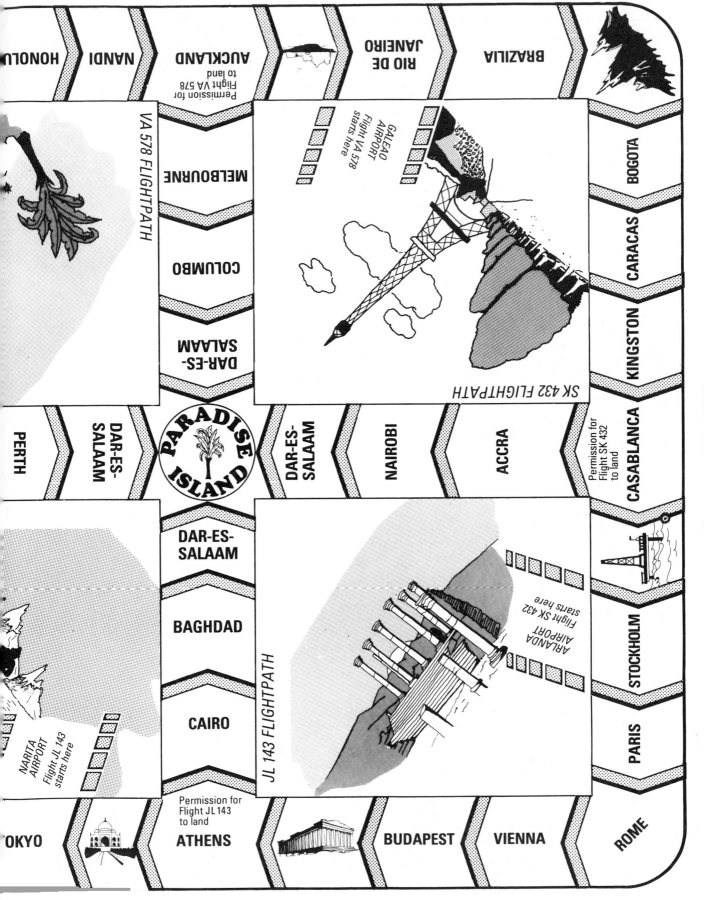

HONOLU

NANDI

AUCKLAND

Permission for Flight VA 578 to land

RIO DE JANEIRO

BRAZILIA

BOGOTA

CARACAS

KINGSTON

CASABLANCA

VA 578 FLIGHTPATH

MELBOURNE

COLUMBO

DAR-ES-SALAAM

GALEAO AIRPORT
Flight VA 578 starts here

SK 432 FLIGHTPATH

Permission for Flight SK 432 to land

PERTH

DAR-ES-SALAAM

PARADISE ISLAND

DAR-ES-SALAAM

NAIROBI

ACCRA

STOCKHOLM

DAR-ES-SALAAM

BAGHDAD

CAIRO

ARLANDA AIRPORT
Flight SK 432 starts here

PARIS

NARITA AIRPORT
Flight JL 143 starts here

JL 143 FLIGHTPATH

ROME

OKYO

Permission for Flight JL 143 to land

ATHENS

BUDAPEST

VIENNA

HOW TO SAY IT

(*OE* = Oral Exercise; *Ext* = Extension exercise)

FUNCTION		EXAMPLE SENTENCE	UNIT: *Set*
Advise	Give instructions and advice	*Lock the doors.*	7:4
		Don't leave the windows open.	
Agree and disagree	Agree with suggestions	*That's a good idea!*	2:3
	Disagree with suggestions	*I'm not so keen on swimming.*	2:3
	Agree to a request	*(Could you get me some milk?) Yes, sure.*	7:3
		(May I come and see the flat?) Yes, of course.	5:1
	Agree to do things	*(Remember to lock the door.) I will. Don't worry.*	9:2
	Agree positively	*Yes, I'm sure she will.|Yes, so do I.|Yes, I do, too.|*	15:2
		No, I'm sure she won't.|Neither do I.|Nor do I.| I don't either.	
	Agree neutrally	*Well, maybe she will.|Mmm, possibly.|Perhaps.|*	15:2
		Well, maybe she won't.|Mmm, possibly not.	
	Disagree	*No, she won't!|Do you? I don't.|Well, I*	
		don't think she will.|Yes, she will!|	
		Don't you? I do.|Well, I think she will.	
Apologise	Apologise and give an explanation	*Sorry I didn't telephone, but I forgot.*	12:1
	Accept apology	*Oh, that's all right. Forget it!*	12:1
	Apologise for not completing activities	*Not yet, I'm afraid. I'm just going to look there.*	13:*OE3*
Ask for personal information	Ask for personal information	*What's your name?*	1
	about present life	*Where are you living now?*	10:1
	about experiences	*Have you ever been to Italy?*	12:3
	about physical appearance	*What does she look like?*	13:1
	about people's past lives	*When were you born?*	14:1
		How long have you been living in Bristol?	
Ask for factual information	Ask about facilities	*Is there a swimming pool here?*	4:1
	for directions	*How do I get to Oak Street?*	4:2
	what people have got	*What have we got?|Have we got any milk?*	7:1
	where things are	*Where's the mayonnaise?*	7:2
	about travel arrangements	*How will we get to the airport?*	15:1
Ask about events	Ask about the recent past	*Did you have a nice weekend? What did you do?*	3:2
	about present actions	*What are you doing? Are you busy?*	8:1
	about plans	*Where are you going to go for your holiday?*	9:1
	about past actions	*What did you do yesterday?*	13:2
	about completed actions	*Have you been to the theatre recently?*	13:3
Ask in social contexts	Ask about likes and dislikes	*Do you like|mind cooking?*	2:1
	for an opinion	*What do you think of Bristol?*	2:2
	about personal comfort and health	*What's the matter? How do you feel today?*	3:1
	for permission	*May|Can I use the telephone?*	5:1
	people to do things	*Could you get me some milk?*	7:3
	about the weather	*What's the weather like today?*	9:3
Check	Check directions	*I see. I turn left and then right.*	4:*OE6*
	Check facts about people	*Your name's Clive, isn't it?*	10:2
Comment	Comment on people's health	*Oh, good! I am glad.|Oh, I am sorry.*	3:1
	on colours	*Mmm. A yellow kitchen. That sounds nice.*	5:*OE4*
	on the weather	*Oh, dear! That's rather cold.*	9:3
	on predictions	*Well, maybe she will.|No, I'm sure she won't.*	15:1
Compare	Make comparisons	*Milan is bigger than I expected.*	
		Florence is more beautiful than Milan.	12:2
Confirm	Confirm excuses	*Yes, I have got a very bad headache.*	8:*OE3*
	facts	*Yes, that's right. It is.*	10:2
	dates	*Right. I was born in 1955.*	14:*OE1*
Correct	Give correct information	*No, Jack's office is here.*	1:*OE4*
		No, no, not Manchester. Bristol.	10:*OE2*
		No, he doesn't actually. He works in Bristol.	10:2
		No, that was when he died.	14:*OE5*
Describe	Describe where places are	*Brighton is situated on the south coast.*	1
	people's likes and dislikes	*Maria likes reading but doesn't like cooking.*	2:1
	facilities	*As well as a cinema, there's a theatre.*	4:1
	a house and furniture	*There are three rooms upstairs.*	5:2
		The curtains are red and white checked.	

FUNCTION		EXAMPLE SENTENCE	UNIT: *Set*
	Describe exactly where things are	*It's in the small cupboard on the top shelf.*	7:2
	a picture	*There's Mr Potter. He's washing up.*	8:*Ext1*
	the weather	*It's warm and sunny.*	9:1
	present lives	*Barbara is studying shoe design.*	10:1
	experiences and impressions	*I went there last summer. It was marvellous.*	12:3
	people's appearance	*He's got red hair. He's wearing jeans.*	13:1
	past life	*I was born in 1955. My father was a miner.*	14:1,2
Direct	Ask for directions	*Excuse me. How do I get to Oak Street?*	4:2
	Give directions	*You walk down Birch Street as far as the traffic lights. Then cross over and turn right.*	4:2
Excuse	Make excuses	*I'm afraid I've got a bad cold.*	8:2
		I'm afraid I've got to do some work.	
		I'm afraid I ought to do my washing.	
		I'm afraid I'd like to go to bed early.	
	Repeat excuses	*I'd love to but I really would like to go to bed early tonight.*	8:*OE5*
Explain	Apologise and give an explanation	*I'm sorry I'm late, but I missed the train.*	12:1
Instruct	Give directions	*Walk down Bond Street. Then turn left.*	4:2
	Give instructions	*Don't lie in the sun for hours.*	7:4
		First peel the potatoes. Then boil them.	
Invite	Invite people to do things	*Would you like to go out for a meal?*	8:2
	Refuse invitations politely	*That's very kind of you, but I'm afraid I've got a bad cold.*	8:2
Narrate	Narrate routine activities	*Yesterday, Wilma Gibson, the swimming champion, got up at 6.30. Then she . . .*	3:2
	Narrate and link past events	*While she was waiting for her flight, she bought a magazine. When the plane took off, she felt nervous.*	12:4
	Narrate recent activities	*Peter has been to the cinema recently and . . .*	13:3
Plan	Make suggestions and plans	*What/How about meeting for lunch?*	2:3
	Agree with plans	*Fine! That's a great idea.*	2:3
	Disagree with plans	*I'm not so keen on lunch. How about supper instead?*	2:3
	Ask and talk about plans	*Where are you going to stay?*	9:1
		We're going to stay in a hotel.	
	Plan travel arrangements	*A company car will pick you up at 8 a.m.*	15:1
Predict	Make predictions	*Everyone will live in cities.*	15:2
		I'll miss all my friends.	
	Comment on predictions	*Yes, I'm sure you will./Well, perhaps you'll miss them a bit./No, you won't!*	15:2
	Question predictions	*Do you really think I will/won't?*	15:*OE6*
Reason	Ask for and give reasons	*Why does Rod like England?*	1
		Because it's so different from Canada.	
		Rod doesn't know many people so he enjoyed meeting Barbara.	
	Refuse permission and give reasons	*(May/Can I use your phone?)*	5:1
		Well, actually,/Sorry, but I'm expecting a phone call myself.	
Refuse	Refuse permission formally	*(May I open the window?)*	5:1
		Well, actually, I've got an awful cold.	
	Refuse permission informally	*(Can I borrow your car?) Sorry, but I need it myself.*	5:1
	Refuse an invitation	*Thanks very much. I'd love to but I've got to work.*	8:2
Remind	Remind people to do things	*You'll remember to lock the door, won't you?*	9:2
		You won't forget to lock the door, will you?	
	Respond to reminders	*Yes, I will./No, I won't. Don't worry.*	9:2
Request	Request permission formally	*May I use the telephone?*	5:1
	Request permission informally	*Can I use the telephone?*	5:1
	Request people to do things formally	*Could you possibly give me a lift, please?*	7:3
	Request people to do things informally	*Give me a lift to the station, please.*	7:*OE5*
Suggest	Make suggestions	*What/How about having a meal at Franco's?*	2:3
	Agree with suggestions	*That's a good/great idea!*	2:3
	Disagree with suggestions	*I'm not so keen on having a meal.*	2:3
	Make alternative suggestions	*Why don't we go to the cinema instead?*	2:3
	Sympathise and suggest remedies	*(I've got a headache.)*	3:1
		Oh, dear! Why don't you lie down for a bit?	

WORD FIELDS

The figure in **bold** beside each word tells you in which unit the word first appears for you to learn it. *v* = verb. SS tells you that the word first appeared in Starting Strategies.

Accommodation
flat SS 4
hotel SS 5
hostel SS 6
room SS 6
guest house 9
villa 9
guest 5
key 5
rent 1, 5
reserve *v* SS 6
stay *v* SS 15

Body and Health
nose 10
ear 10
head 3
face 10
hip 3
leg 3
back 3
shoulder 3
stomach 3
throat 10
hair 8
cold 3
ill SS 16
sick 3
sore (throat) 8
pain 3
temperature 3
headache 3
better 3
comfortable SS 16
aspirin 3
specialist 19
operation 3
accident 3
break *v* 3
feel *v* 3
go to bed *v* SS 19
look (ill) *v* 3
relax *v* 3
stay at home *v* SS 15

Clothes
shoe 1
boot 13
sandals 13
trousers 13
jeans 13
skirt 13
tights 13
belt 13
blouse 13
shirt 13
sweater 13
cardigan 13
dress 13
jacket 13

coat 5
raincoat 13
T-shirt SS 15
ribbon 13
style 13
type 13
modern SS 10
old-fashioned 2
long-sleeved 13
short-sleeved 13
sleeveless 13
bare 9

Colours
beige 5
black SS 11
blue 5
brown 5
green 5
grey 5
orange 5
pink 5
purple 5
yellow 5
dark 5
light 5

Education
(See also Starting
Strategies '*School*')
college SS 19
competition 14
comprehensive school 14
degree 10
economics 14
history 14
play truant *v* 13
sociology 13
successful 14

Emotions and Feelings
bored 15
calm 13
excited 15
miserable 3
nervous 12
glad 3
feel *v* 3
hate *v* 2
care *v* 15
hope *v* 10
miss (someone) *v* 12
smile *v* 10
relief 12
row 15

*Facilities: Shops and
Services*
(See also Starting
Strategies '*Places and*

Buildings'; '*Shops and
Shopping*')
bank SS 5
bus stop 4
car park SS 6
chemist 4
church SS 16
cinema SS 5
hairdresser 4
hospital SS 19
hotel SS 5
launderette 4
library 4
museum 4
newsagent 5
off licence 4
park SS 1
post office SS 5
pub SS 19
restaurant SS 5
shopping centre SS 5
station SS 5
sweet shop 7
swimming pool 4
supermarket SS 5
theatre SS 16
traffic lights 4
transport 4
travel agency 4

Food
(See also Starting
Strategies '*Food, Drink
and Meals*')
diet 7
flour 7
ham 7
jam 7
juice 15
mayonnaise 7
olive oil 7
onion 7
parsley 7
pepper 7
recipe 7
rice 7
snack 15
sweets 7

Furniture
(See also Starting
Strategies '*Rooms and
Furniture*')
armchair 5
bookcase 5
carpet 5
chair 5
cooker 5
curtain 5
desk 5

drawer 7
dressing table 5
fridge 5
lamp 5
shelf 7
sink 5
sofa 5
table SS 6
wardrobe 5
cupboard 5
washbasin 5
tap 5
ceiling 5
floor 5
stairs 3
wall 5
central heating 5

Household objects
bowl 7
fork 7
knife 7
spoon 7
saucer 7
cup SS 10
saucepan 7
blanket 7
sheet 7
towel 7
vacuum cleaner 7
leather 5
plastic 5
material 5
metal 5
wood 5

Leisure activities
spare time 1
pleasure 1
interest 1
carpentry 12
dressmaking 12
gymnastics 12
squash 12
fish *v* 2
climb *v* 9
sail *v* 12
play cards *v* 8
chat *v* 8
entertain *v* 8
enjoy *v* 1

Occupations and Work
(See also Starting
Strategies '*Occupations*')
air steward(ess) 2
architect 2
carpenter 10
cashier 9
composer 14

computer operator 2
customs officer 14
dentist 12
designer 12
diver 13
folk singer 14
librarian 10
manager 1
manageress 1
miner 14
novelist 14
nurse 2
personnel officer 15
policeman(woman) 2
pop star 14
representative 15
social worker 12
travel guide 2
branch 10
docks 14
firm 10
oil rig 10
factory SS 19
pop group 14
shoe shop 1
component 14
design 9
electrical 1
production 1
shift work 2
uniform 2
become v 10
build v 10
change job v 14
train v 2
do well v 10

Place and position
(See also Starting
Strategies '*Places*';
Prepositions)
canal 13
capital 9
city 1
coast 1
countryside 2
field 9
lane 9
mountain 1
square 4
village 2
above 7
at the end of 4
beside 7
between 4
bottom 7
corner 4
edge 13
half way down 4
left 4
middle 7
nearest 4
right 4

the other side of 2
top 5
under 7
come from v 1
cross over v 4
situated 1

Qualities
attractive 2
depressing 2
dirty 12
dull 2
easy-going 7
exciting 5
fashionable 9
kind 7
lively 7
loving 13
marvellous 2
old-fashioned 2
religious 14
real 14
sweet 3
ugly 2
unfriendly 2
wild 13
fast 10
slow 2
great 2
large 5
high 5
long 2
tall 12
wide 12
hard 5
soft 5
low 5
noisy 5
round 5
a bit 2
sense of humour 7
talent 14

Time
(See also Starting
Strategies '*Time*')
already 9
at present 10
first 3
for once 8
later on 8
some other time 8
then 3
after 3
ago 14
at the end of 4
since 14
until 3
at a bad time 8
spare time 1
still 9
immediate 15
urgent 13

just 8
future 9
fortnight 9

Travel
airport SS 6
air terminal SS 6
centre (city) SS 6
plane SS 13
check-in desk 12
passport control 12
customs 12
departure lounge 12
ticket SS 14
suitcase SS 14
luggage 12
baggage allowance 15
trolley 12
seat belt 12
travellers' cheques 7
money 7
currency 15
franc 15
flight SS 13
trip 9
on business 4
arrive v SS 13
leave v SS 13
check in v 12
go abroad v 14
get to v SS 18
meet v SS 7
slow down v 12
hitch-hike v 9
lie in the sun v 7
sunbathe v 7
boat 9

Weather
(See also Starting
Strategies '*Weather*')
spring 2
summer 2
autumn 2
winter 2
temperature SS 9
centigrade 9
degree 9
high 5
low 5
calm 3
cold SS 9
cool 12
dark 5
dull 2
mild 2
cloudy 9
foggy 9
windy 9
rain v 9
snow 9
sun 9
raincoat 9

umbrella 2

Verbs: mental operations
check 9
count 9
decide 13
expect 13
forget 9
guess SS 7
hope 10
know 1
learn SS 11
prefer SS 19
realise 13
remember SS 16
think of 2

Verbs: routine activities
(See also Starting Strategies
'*Daily Routine Activities*')
borrow 5
buy SS 14
cancel (the newspaper) 9
catch (post/train) 10
collect 9
cook SS 11
do some homework SS 19
do the housework SS 19
do the ironing SS 19
do some shopping SS 14
do the washing-up 2
drink SS 14
drive SS 14
eat SS 14
fasten 9
get up SS 19
go out for a meal SS 15
go to bed SS 19
go to sleep SS 16
go to work SS 19
have breakfast SS 19
lend 5
listen to SS 19
look after 2
make sure 15
organise 2
paint 5
pick up 9
put somebody to bed 8
read SS 19
rush 10
serve 5
turn on 5
turn out 9
use 5
wash 5
wash (my hair) 8
watch TV SS 15
write SS 11

WORD LIST

The figure in **bold** beside each word tells you in which unit the word first appears for you to learn it. v = verb.

A
a bit 2
above 7
accident 3
after 3
ago 14
air 12
air steward(ess) 2
alcohol 3
alive 14
allowance 15
alone 2
already 9
another 1
anymore 10
anything 7
appearance 13
apply v 15
application 15
architect 2
armchair 5
arrangements 15
aspirin 3
as well as 4
at a bad time 8
at present 10
at the end of 4
atomic 15
attractive 2
autumn 2

B
baby 8
back 3
background 14
bad 8
baggage allowance 15
bare 9
because 1
become v 10
begin v 14
Be good! 10
beige 5
belt 13
beside 7
bestseller 14
better 3
between 4
bit 7
blanket 7
blouse 13
blue 5
boat 9
bookcase 5
boots 13
born (be born) 14
borrow v 5
boss 5
bother v 15
bottom 7
bowl 7

branch 9
break v 3
brown 5
build v 10
business (on business) 4
bus stop 4
busy 8
by the way 1

C
calm 13
canal 13
cancel v 9
capital 9
card 8
cardigan 13
care v 15
career 12
carpenter 10
carpentry 12
carpet 5
carry v 7
cashier 9
catch v 10
ceiling 5
celebrate v 15
centigrade 9
central heating 5
Certainly! 5
chair 5
change 2
change v 14
chat 8
check v 9
checked 5
check in v 12
check-in desk 12
chemist 4
choose v 2
city 1
climb v 9
cloudy 9
coast 1
coat 5
cold 3
collect v 9
combine v 14
come from v 1
commune 15
competition 14
component 1
composer 14
comprehensive school 14
computer operator 2
contact v 13
cooker 5
cool 12
copy v 7
corner 4
cottage 1
cough 8

count v 9
countryside 2
cross over v 4
cupboard 5
curly 13
currency 15
curtain 5
customs 12
customs officer 14
cut v 7

D
dark 5
daughter 1
dead/died 14
decide v 13
definitely 8
degree (temperature) 9
degree (education) 10
dentist 12
departure lounge 12
depend (it depends) 2
depressing 2
design 9
designer 9
desk 5
detective 14
diet (on a . . .) 7
dirty 12
disco 4
discuss v 10
diver 13
divide v 9
Do! 5
docks 14
Don't bother 15
do well 10
do our best 13
drawer 7
dress 13
dressmaking 12
drown v 13
dull 2

E
ear 10
earn v 14
easygoing 7
economics 14
edge 13
either 15
electrical 1
enclose v 15
end 4
energetic 12
energy 15
engaged 15·
enjoy v 1
essential 4
entertain v 8
entertainment 4

escape 13
even (not even) 4
except for 4
exception 4
excited 15
exciting 5
expect (a child) v 10
expect v 13
explain v 9

F
face 10
facility 4
fall (fell) v 13
fashionable 9
fast 10
fasten v 9
fatal 13
feel v 3
fence 13
few 4
fictional 14
field 9
firm 10
first 3
fish v 12
floor 5
flour 7
flowery 5
foggy 9
folk singer 14
football ground 4
forget v 9
fork 7
for once 8
fortnight 9
franc 15
fridge 5
fringe 13
fun 8
future 9

G
get off v 4
get up to date v 10
girlfriend 7
glad 3
go abroad v 14
great 2
green 5
grey 5
group 14
grow up v 14
guard v 9
guest 5
guest house 9
guide v 14
gymnastics 14

H
hair 8

hairdresser 4
half 5
half way down 4
ham 7
hand 5
hard 5
hate v 2
have a look round v 2
headache 3
healthy 3
hear v 10
heavy 5
here 1
high 5
high (price) 5
hip 3
his 1
history 14
hit 14
hitch-hike v 9
hope v 10
humour (sense of humour) 7

I
immediate 15
in 7
instant (coffee) 10
interest 1
It depends 2
It was nice meeting you! 10

J
jacket 13
jam 7
jeans 13
just 8

K
keep v 11
key 5
knife 7
know v 1

L
lamp 5
lane 9
large 5
later on 8
launch 13
launderette 4
leather 5
left 4
leg 3
lend v 5
lettuce 7
librarian 10
library 4
lie v 7
life (way of life) 2
light (colour) 5
light (weight) 5

IRREGULAR VERBS IN STARTING STRATEGIES AND BUILDING STRATEGIES

These verbs are in their **infinitive**/past tense/*past participle* forms.

Verbs with no change

cost	cost	*cost*
cut	cut	*cut*
hit	hit	*hit*
let	let	*let*
put	put	*put*
shut	shut	*shut*

Verbs with one change

bring	brought	*brought*
build	built	*built*
buy	bought	*bought*
catch	caught	*caught*
feel	felt	*felt*
find	found	*found*
get	got	*got*
have	had	*had*
hear	heard	*heard*
keep	kept	*kept*
learn	learnt	*learnt*
leave	left	*left*
lend	lent	*lent*
lose	lost	*lost*
make	made	*made*
mean	meant	*meant*
meet	met	*met*
oversleep	overslept	*overslept*
pay	paid	*paid*
read	read [red]	*read* [red]
say	said	*said*
sell	sold	*sold*
send	sent	*sent*
sit	sat	*sat*
tell	told	*told*
think	thought	*thought*
understand	understood	*understood*

Verbs with two changes

be	was	*been*
begin	began	*begun*
break	broke	*broken*
choose	chose	*chosen*
come	came	*come*
do	did	*done*
drink	drank	*drunk*
drive	drove	*driven*
eat	ate	*eaten*
fall	fell	*fallen*
forget	forgot	*forgotten*
give	gave	*given*
go	went	*gone*
grow	grew	*grown*
know	knew	*known*
lie	lay	*lain*
ride	rode	*ridden*
ring	rang	*rung*
see	saw	*seen*
show	showed	*shown*
sing	sang	*sung*
speak	spoke	*spoken*
swim	swam	*swum*
take	took	*taken*
wear	wore	*worn*
write	wrote	*written*

ACKNOWLEDGEMENTS

We are grateful to the following for permission to reproduce textual and recorded copyright material:

The author's agent and the author Roald Dahl for an adapted extract from the short story "The Landlady" from *Kiss Kiss* published by Michael Joseph Ltd and Penguin Books Ltd.

The extract "Warning Hints" on page 50 is from *How to Live in Britain* published by Longman for the British Council. The extract "Do's and Don'ts" on page 50 from *The Traveller's Guide* published by The National Westminster Bank.

We are grateful to the following for permission to reproduce copyright photographs:

Barnaby's Picture Library for page 37; Lance Browne for page 10 (top left); Camera Press Ltd., for pages 9–10 (bottom), 111, 118 (bottom right); Conservative Central Office for page 10 (middle); Hoa-Qui Agency for page 79; Reproduced by kind permission of the Home Office for page 67 (middle); Keystone Press Agency Ltd, for pages 10 (bottom right), 118 (top); Mary Evans Picture Library for page 127; Mike Millman (Sea Angler Magazine) for page 87 (left); Guernica by Pablo Picasso, on extended loan to the Museum of Modern Art, New York for page 10 (top right); National Theatre (photo by James Holmes) for page 9 (top); Peter Baker Photography for page 9–10 (top left); Reproduced by kind permission of the Royal Society for the Prevention of Accidents for page 67 (top & bottom); Sunday Telegraph for page 14; Syndication International Ltd., for page 118 (bottom left); John Walmsley for page 17–18; Janine Wiedel for page 27.

We have been unable to trace the copyright holder of the photograph on page 10 (bottom left), and would be grateful for any information that would enable us to do so.

Illustrated by:

Malcolm Bird page 8; Malcolm Stokes page 12; Graham Round page 20; Clive Spong pages 25/26; 35/36, 48; Terry Rogers pages 49, 87; Keith Rawling page 55; Belinda Lyon page 60; Mike Bell page 65; Geoffrey Hart Associates page 88; John Walsh page 89; Sally Kindberg page 91; Mike Tregenza page 117; Carol Tarrant pages 125/126; Valerie Sangster page 127 top.

Situational photographs throughout, taken by Chris Moyse.

And thanks to all those who helped as models and who provided locations for the story photographs.